Teacher's Book of Plays and Choral Readings

Macmillan/McGraw-Hill School Publishing Company

New York   Chicago   Columbus

Contents

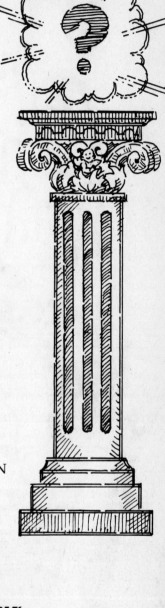

WRITE YOUR OWN

CHORAL READINGS

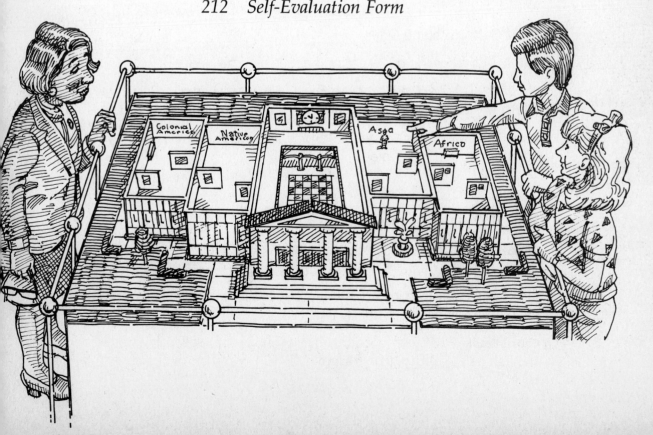

Correlations

Unit Themes, Plays, and Choral Readings

Each play and choral reading selection has been developed to reinforce the unit theme in the Student Anthology

Level 11

Unit 1 Unforgettable Places

Theme: Memorable places both real and imaginary

Play: *Castles and Quests*—a medieval fantasy in which two children discover that the setting of a new computer game is more realistic than they ever imagined

Choral Reading: *Goblin Feet*—a poem that describes a place so enchanting that it can never be forgotten

Unit 2 Transformations

Theme: Things change: internally, external, functionally

Play: *The Breath of Life*—a suspenseful dramatization of the heroic rescue efforts of black inventor Garrett Morgan and others during the Cleveland Water Works tunnel disaster of 1916

Choral Reading: *The Snowflake* and *Today*—poems about physical transformations wrought by the weather

Unit 3 Against the Odds

Theme: Overcoming obstacles and accepting challenges

Play: *The Case of the Uncooked Eggs*—an adaptation of a Haitian folk tale in which a gift presents an unexpected challenge to the recipient

Choral Reading: *Measure Me, Sky* and *Youth*—poems that issue a joyous challenge to young people

Unit 4 Getting to Know You

Theme: Developing relationships and understandings

Play: *Dog Gone*—a contemporary play in which everyone, including the family pet, deals with the adjustment that occurs when two households are merged into one new family unit

Choral Reading: *Writers*—a poem that describes the relationship between two friends as expressed in their different writing styles

Unit 5 Way to Go

Theme: Journeys to discoveries

Play: *'Round the World with Nellie Bly*—a dramatization of a young newspaper reporter's record-setting trip around the world in the days before jet planes, international telephone service, or wash-and-wear clothing

Choral Reading: *Crossing*—a poem that celebrates travel by rail

Unit 6 Are You Sure?

Theme: Asking questions and becoming a critical thinker

Play: *The Museum Exhibit Case*—things and people aren't necessarily what they seem in this mystery caper that is solved by careful logic and deductive reasoning

Choral Reading: *A Cliché*—a poem in which the reader is invited to think again about some trite expressions

Introduction

We read for many different reasons, but chief among them should be the discovery that reading can be both fun and purposeful. And what could be more entertaining than working together to make words come alive in a Readers Theater or choral-reading presentation? This book of plays and choral readings has been developed to give you and your students an opportunity to enjoy reading aloud together. At the same time, your students will be developing their reading fluency skills through these enjoyable and motivating oral-reading experiences.

The following pages provide a compilation of hints and tips gathered from teachers who have made oral-reading techniques work in their classrooms. Unlike dramatic productions requiring memorization, elaborate sets, costumes, and stage directions, Readers Theater and choral reading only require a set of scripts and a group of enthusiastic readers—the former you are holding, while the latter wait in the wings of your classroom!

READERS THEATER—A DESCRIPTION

Readers Theater has been used by teachers for many years. Also known as Dramatic Reading, Chamber Theater, or Story Theater, the name Readers Theater seems most appropriate because it puts the emphasis where it belongs—on the *reading* rather than the memorization of a script. Unlike traditional drama in which performers memorize lines and move about a stage, Readers Theater is simply the rehearsed oral reading of a script by a group of performers. It requires no training in drama or the performing arts on the part of students or teachers; there are no complicated guidelines to follow. While simple costumes or backdrops can be used to help establish characterization and setting, they are optional. The fact that Readers Theater involves such simple techniques makes it a viable option for every classroom.

READERS THEATER AND CHORAL READING—THE BENEFITS

Among the chief benefits of Readers Theater and choral reading is the development of oral-reading fluency. Identified by some reading authorities as a frequently "neglected goal" of reading instruction, fluency training has been recognized as an important aspect of proficient reading.

Two essential components for successful fluency training are repeated reading and active listening. Most students can sharpen their active listening skills by attending while the teacher reads aloud for a brief period every day. However, convincing students to repeatedly read the same selection orally until fluency is achieved is quite a different matter. Usually the response is less than enthusiastic.

Enter Readers Theater and choral reading!— both natural partners for fluency training. The oral reading of plays and poetry generates a natural excitement and a willingness to rehearse that enables teachers to integrate repeated reading practice into their instructional program. The goal of a polished performance is a genuinely motivating force that provides a rationale for the fluency training that all students need. Readers Theater and choral reading offer students a *meaningful* context in which to practice expression, shading, phrasing, diction, pitch, and rate, as well as word recognition skills. (For additional information on fluency training and its benefits, see the articles listed in the Bibliography.)

Readers Theater and choral reading also develop active listening skills on the part of both participants and audience. Readers must listen attentively to pick up on cues or to chime in as a member of a group. Audience members also are encouraged to sharpen listening skills as they interpret the dialog and narration to visualize settings and characters that are described rather than visibly presented on stage.

In addition to developing fluency skills, Readers Theater and choral reading can also help students internalize literature, thereby improving their comprehension. Dramatizations enable readers to "become" the characters they play. What better way to reinforce character and plot development than through plays? Dramatizations also expose students to the rich heritage of oral language and storytelling. Through the oral reading of scripts and poetry, students internalize the rhythm of repeated refrains, certain language conventions, and traditional story structure.

A final benefit of Readers Theater and choral reading is derived from the high levels of student interaction and involvement within cooperative learning groups. Through these shared oral-reading experiences, students learn to work together, take turns, listen to each other, and employ group decision-making and problem-solving strategies in casting and production decisions.

Unlike many group activities in which all participants must function on or about the same level to effectively complete the task, a Readers Theater group using the scripts in this book can be composed of students with widely differing reading abilities. The scripts have been written to include roles of varying length and difficulty, enabling students of all ability levels to fully participate and contribute to the achievement of the common goal: a shared oral-reading experience.

LAUNCHING READERS THEATER IN YOUR CLASSROOM

As the following steps indicate, introducing Readers Theater to your class is a straightforward procedure. The only rules are: Keep it simple! and Keep it fun!

1. SCRIPT PREPARATION

Decide when you want to introduce the Readers Theater play within a unit. Then duplicate a copy of the script for each cast member and the director. (Since scripts sometimes have a habit of disappearing, you might make a few extras, just in case.) Students can make construction-paper covers, using the full-page art that precedes each script for decoration, if they wish.

2. ROLE ASSIGNMENT

The plays in this collection were purposefully written with roles requiring varying levels of reading proficiency. Initially you may want to take into account individual reading ability when making role assignments, but once students have become familiar with a play, roles can and should be switched. Because the characters are read rather than acted, the part of a boy can be read by a girl and vice versa.

As students become familiar with Readers Theater, they should be encouraged to assume responsibility for casting decisions as they participate within the cooperative decision-making environment of a Readers Theater group.

3. REHEARSALS

In the first rehearsal, students in the cast should sit together in a Readers Theater group—perhaps gathered around a table—and read through the script to get a sense of the plot and characters. If the play is an adaptation, you may want to read aloud the original story. (Sources for stories that have been adapted appear in the Bibliography.) At this time, roles should be assigned or agreed upon, and students can be encouraged to identify their lines with a transparent highlighter.

Subsequent rehearsals should include paired repeated readings where two characters rehearse their lines together. Having a tape recorder available for these readings will enable students to evaluate their progress. In these early rehearsals, students should focus on word recognition and on listening for cues. Once these goals have been achieved, attention can be turned to articulation, expression, rate, shading, and phrasing. Invite students to make "reader's notes" in pencil in their scripts. A slash, for example, can be used as a reminder of a pause not indicated by punctuation. An underline can indicate that a word needs special emphasis. These notations can be a valuable aid to oral reading.

During rehearsals, students may decide to add their own personal touches to a script. If the cast decides to add, delete, or alter a speech, this change should be made in all copies of the script.

4. BLOCKING AND FOCUS

In Readers Theater, the performers usually do not move about the stage. However, there are two bits of "stage business" that require rehearsal—where the performers will sit in relation to each other, and where they should look when they are speaking.

Each play is accompanied by a blocking diagram that suggests a seating arrangement. Before the performance, students will need to practice entering, assuming their places on stools or chairs, and exiting. If music stands are available, you may wish to have students use them to hold their scripts during a performance. In some cases, a music stand for the narrator has been suggested in the blocking diagram.

Focus should be an important part of the rehearsal process because, with the exception of a simple gesture or two, focus is the only direct action employed during a Readers Theater presentation. Basically, there are two kinds of focus that students can use: on-stage and off-stage focus. In on-stage focus, the characters look at each other when they speak. In off-stage focus, the characters direct their gaze to a spot on the wall behind the audience. In both types of focus, it is important that students be familiar enough with their lines so their eyes and heads are up rather than buried in a script.

5. PROPS AND COSTUMES

While elaborate costumes and props are not necessary for Readers Theater, even the simplest costumes, such as hats, scarves, or animal ears can help students assume their character. Costume suggestions can be found on the resource pages following several of the plays.

Making background murals or very simple props can help students deepen their understanding of a play. Involvement in discussions about what to emphasize in a drawing or in the scenery or about which free-standing props would suggest the setting (a tree) or occasion (a birthday cake) allows a further involvement and commitment on the part of participants. Either the performers or another group of students acting as stage crew can create the props and costumes.

Hand-held props are not suggested for Readers Theater because the hands should be free to hold the script. For a similar reason, masks should be avoided since they may impair the performers' ability to see the script or project the lines.

6. THE STAGE

Readers Theater does not require a proscenium stage with a curtain, just an open area with enough space for the cast and an audience. A corner of the classroom will work as well as the school auditorium. For plays that lend themselves to puppet dramatizations, simple directions for both the puppets and the stage are included in the resource pages. In staging a Readers Theater puppet show, it generally works best to have one cast read the script while another cast operates the puppets.

7. SHARING THE PERFORMANCE

Readers Theater presentations are meant to be shared, but the audience can range from one person to a packed auditorium. Before the performance begins, you or a student may wish to briefly introduce the conventions of Readers Theater so that the audience understands its role in interpreting dialog to visualize the characters and the action. Students may enjoy making programs, tickets, and posters for the production, especially if another class or parents are invited to attend. On the day of the performance, have the characters enter, take their places, and read!

8. PERFORMANCE FOLLOW-UP

After the performance, suggest that the cast gather to discuss their reading of the play. To guide their discussion, they may use the Self-Evaluation Form. By assessing their own performances as readers, as listeners, and as group members, students can set personal goals to work toward during their next oral-reading experience.

WRITE YOUR OWN READERS THEATER PLAY

After participating in a Readers Theater performance, some students will be eager to write their own plays. The Write Your Own Readers Theater Play resource pages have been designed to guide students through this process.

The teacher resource page presents an overview of the steps and highlights some of the major differences between narrative and drama. Once students understand those differences, they can work with partners or in small groups to complete the student resource pages.

- *Getting Started* guides students in answering the question, "How do I get an idea for a play?"

- *The Plot* defines plot structure and gives a model of a plot outline. Building on the previous worksheet, students develop their own plot outline based on one of the play ideas previously identified.

- *Creating Characters* discusses methods for developing realistic characters and models how to write character sketches.

- *A Readers Theater Script* illustrates the proper format for a script. Additionally, it focuses attention on key questions involving the role of the narrator and the importance of creating dialog consistent with a character sketch.

- *Ready, Set, Write!* is a writing-process checklist to help students keep track of the steps involved in prewriting, drafting, revising, proofreading, and publishing a Readers Theater play.

THE CHORAL READING EXPERIENCE

Choral reading, like Readers Theater, is an activity that promotes fluency through cooperative effort. In choral reading, speaking and listening are complementary processes—groups of students practice reading poetry for another group to listen to. During practice sessions, the group will need a director, usually the teacher in the early sessions. As students become more experienced with this technique, they can explore taking on the responsibilities of the director.

TYPES OF CHORAL READING

Choral reading promotes fluency by giving support to readers, by providing an opportunity for repeated reading with special attention to rhythm and meter, and by encouraging active listening. The four major types of choral reading are

- refrain
- antiphonal
- line-by-line
- unison

In a poem with a refrain, the verse can be read by a solo voice, by a group (the most common choice), or in combination. In line-by-line choral reading, each line or group of lines is read by a different group or solo voice. Antiphonal choral readings are somewhat like call and response, with one group answering another. Unison readings—perhaps the most difficult of all—are read by the entire group.

The choral readings for each unit have suggestions for groups and solo voices. Your students should first try reading the poems as arranged. After they are familiar with a particular reading, encourage them to try other arrangements or other poems.

SIZE AND ORGANIZATION OF THE CHORAL READING GROUP

You and your students may want to experiment with the size of the choral reading group, which will vary depending upon the number of students who want to participate and the particular piece being performed. Most often, members of a group should stand together. Sometimes, readers with solo parts are also part of a group. In these cases, the soloists should stand in the front row of the group. Resource pages suggest arrangements of speakers for choral reading.

THE RESOURCE PAGES

This book includes both teacher and student resource pages. Resource pages follow the plays and always include a blocking diagram for the play. Other resource pages may include costume suggestions and patterns, a pronunciation guide, prop suggestions, puppets, puppet-show directions, sound effects, and audiotaping instructions for radio plays. Resource pages for the choral readings include blocking diagrams. The final resource page is a self-evaluation form for readers and listeners.

BIBLIOGRAPHY

ARTICLES ON READING FLUENCY

ALLINGTON, R.L. 1983. Fluency: The neglected reading goal. *The Reading Teacher* 36:556-61.
BEAVER, J.M. 1982. Say it! Over and over. *Language Arts* 59:143-48.
DOWHOWER, S.L. 1987. Effects of repeated reading on second-grade transitional readers' fluency and comprehension. *Reading Research Quarterly* 22:389-406.
_____. 1989. Repeated reading: Research into practice. *The Reading Teacher* 42:502-7.
KOSKINEN, P.S., and I.H. BLUM. 1986. Paired repeated reading: A classroom strategy for developing fluent reading. *The Reading Teacher* 40:70-75.
MICCINATI, J.L. 1985. Using prosodic cues to teach oral reading fluency. *The Reading Teacher* 39:206-12.
RASINSKI, T. 1989. Fluency for everyone: Incorporating fluency instruction in the classroom. *The Reading Teacher* 42:690-93.

_____ , and J.B. ZUTELL. 1990. Making a place for fluency instruction in the regular reading curriculum. *Reading Research and Instruction* 29:85-91.

SAMUELS, S.J. 1988. Decoding and automaticity: Helping poor readers become automatic at word recognition. *The Reading Teacher* 41:756-60.

ARTICLES ON READERS THEATER AND DRAMATIC READING

ANDERSEN, D.R. 1987. Around the world in eighty days. *Instructor* 97(October): 62-63.

_____ . 1989. The shy exclamation point. *Instructor* 98(February): 54.

_____ . 1988. The sound of great voices. *Instructor* 97(January): 46-47.

BENNETT, S., and K. BEATTY. 1988. Grades 1 and 2 love readers theatre. *The Reading Teacher* 41:485.

BIDWELL, S.M. 1990. Using drama to increase motivation, comprehension and fluency. *Journal of Reading* 34:38-41.

BURNS, G., and E. KIZER. 1987. Audio-visual effects in readers' theatre: A case study. *International Journal of Instructional Media* 14(3): 223-37.

DICKINSON, E. 1987. Readers Theatre: A creative method to increase reading fluency and comprehension skills. *The New England Reading Association Journal* 23(22): 7-11.

EPPERHEIMER, D. 1991. Readers' Theatre and technology: A perfect mix. *The California Reader* 24(Spring): 14-15.

FREEDMAN, M. 1990. Readers Theatre: An exciting way to motivate reluctant readers. *The New England Reading Association Journal* 26(Autumn): 9-12.

HOWARD, W.L., and others. 1989. Using choral responding to increase active student response. *Teaching Exceptional Children.* 21(Spring): 72-75.

NAVASCUES, M. 1988. Oral and dramatic interpretation of literature in the Spanish class. *Hispania* 71(March): 186-89.

STEWIG, J.W. 1990. Children's books for readers' theatre. *Perspectives* Spring:vii-x.

BOOKS ON READERS THEATER

BAUER, CAROLINE FELLER. *Celebrations: Read-Aloud Holiday and Theme Book Programs.* New York: H.W. Wilson, 1985.

_____ . *Presenting Reader's Theatre: Plays and Poems to Read Aloud.* New York: H.W. Wilson, 1987.

COGER, LESLIE IRENE, and MELVIN R. WHITE. *Readers Theatre Handbook: A Dramatic Approach to Literature.* 3d ed. Glenview, Ill.: Scott, Foresman, 1982.

FORKERT, OTTO MAURICE. *Children's Theatre that Captures Its Audience.* Chicago: Coach House Press, 1962.

LAUGHLIN, MILDRED KNIGHT, and KATHY HOWARD LATROBE. *Readers Theatre for Children*. Englewood, Colo.: Teacher Ideas Press, 1990.

SIERRA, JUDY, and ROBERT KAMINSKI. *Twice Upon a Time: Stories to Tell, Retell, Act Out, and Write About*. New York: H.W. Wilson, 1989.

SLOYER, SHIRLEE. *Readers Theatre: Story Dramatization in the Classroom*. Urbana, Ill.: National Council of Teachers of English, 1982.

_____ . "Readers Theatre: A Reading Motivator." In *Selected Articles on the Teaching of Reading*. New York: Barnell Loft, 1977.

BOOKS ON CHORAL READING

AGGERTT, OTIS J., and ELBERT R. BOWEN. *Communicative Reading*. New York: Macmillan, 1972.

GOTTLIEB, MARVIN R. *Oral Interpretation*. New York: McGraw-Hill, 1980.

JOHNSON, ALBERT, and BERTHA JOHNSON. *Oral Reading: Creative and Interpretive*. South Brunswick: A. S. Barnes, 1971.

BOOKS ON COSTUMES, MAKE-UP, AND PROPS

ARNOLD, A. *Arts and Crafts for Children and Young People*. London: Macmillan, 1976.

BARWELL, EVE. *Disguises You Can Make*. New York: Lothrop, Lee & Shepard, 1977.

CHERNOFF, GOLDIE TAUB. *Easy Costumes You Don't Have to Sew*. New York: Four Winds Press, 1975.

HALEY, GAIL E. *Costumes for Plays and Playing*. New York: Metheun, 1982.

Make and Play Paperback Set (includes costumes, face painting, hats, masks, and T-shirt painting). New York: Franklin Watts, 1990.

McCASLIN, NELLIE. *Shows on a Shoestring: An Easy Guide to Amateur Productions*. New York: David McKay, 1979.

MORIN, ALICE. *Newspaper Theatre: Creative Play Production for Low Budgets and No Budgets*. Belmont, Calif.: Fearon Teacher Aids, 1989.

PARISH, PEGGY. *Costumes to Make*. New York: Macmillan, 1970.

PITCHER, CAROLINE, consultant. *Masks and Puppets*. New York: Franklin Watts, 1984.

PURDY, SUSAN. *Costumes for You to Make*. Philadelphia: J.B. Lippincott, 1971.

SOURCE FOR ADAPTATIONS

"The Case of the Uncooked Eggs," from *The Magic Orange Tree*, collected by Diane Wolkstein, New York: Knopf, 1978.

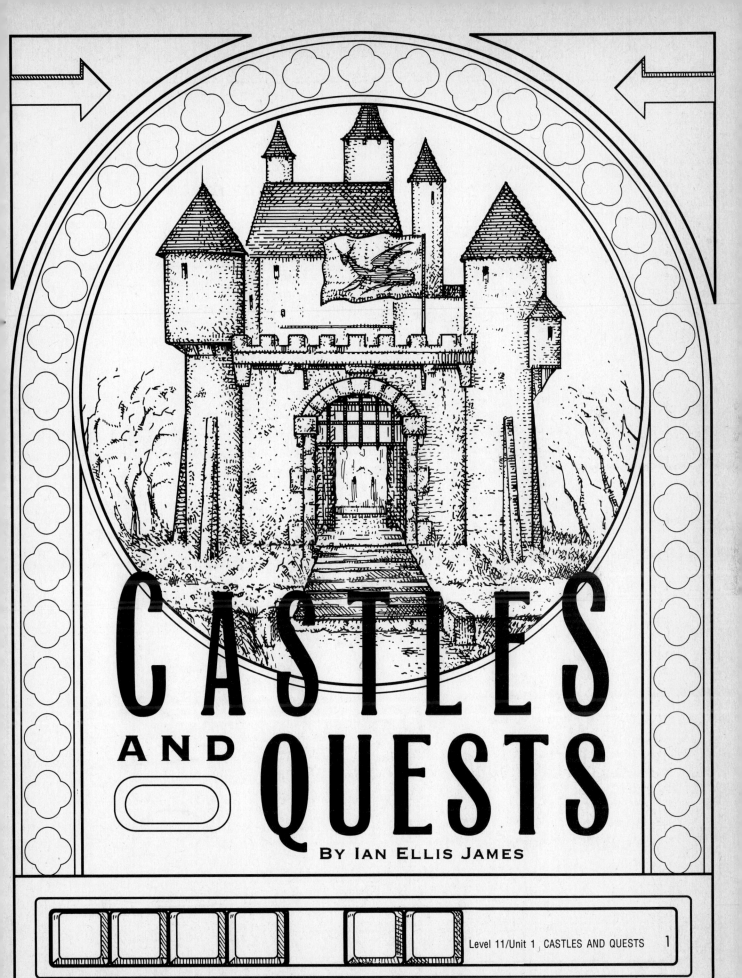

CASTLES
AND QUESTS

By Ian Ellis James

Cast

NARRATOR	MAGE OF MIRTH
VICTOR	TROLL
MR. HILL	ORC
MARITZA	DRAGON
COMPUTER	GOBLIN 1
KNIGHT OF LIGHT	GOBLIN 2
MISTRESS OF SONG	

Macmillan/McGraw-Hill

NARRATOR: It was a wet Saturday in November. Victor, who had just celebrated his tenth birthday, was headed for Mr. Hill's toy store to spend what remained of his birthday loot.

VICTOR: Hi, Mr. Hill.

MR. HILL: Hi, Victor, long time no see! How are things going? I guess school must be keeping you pretty busy.

VICTOR: Yeah, school and music and sports are all keeping me busy! At least we're doing some pretty neat stuff this year, especially in social studies.

MR. HILL: Really? What kind of stuff?

VICTOR: Oh, we're studying about the Middle Ages—you know, knights, squires, manors, and that sort of thing.

MR. HILL: Sounds pretty exciting, all right. Speaking of the Middle Ages, I have a castle kit over in the model section that might be of interest to you.

VICTOR: Actually, what I'm really looking for is a computer game. You see, I got some money for my birthday. My mom made me save half of it, but I have $15 left. I was wondering if you had any computer games for that amount.

MR. HILL: Gosh, Victor, you're welcome to look at what I have, but most of the computer games start around $30 and go up from there. I don't think I have anything in the price range you're talking about. Why don't you look through the display rack over there while I check the stock behind the register.

VICTOR: Thanks, Mr. Hill.

NARRATOR: Mr. Hill pulled a ladder out from behind the door and climbed up to look at the games stored on a high shelf behind the cash register. Meanwhile, Victor looked through the games on the rack.

VICTOR: You were right, Mr. Hill. There's nothing here for under $30. I guess I'll just have to save up and come back another time.

MR. HILL: Hey, look what I found at the very bottom of the stack! Just a minute, and I'll blow the dust off.

SOUND EFFECT: [*blowing sound*]

VICTOR: What is it?

MR. HILL: It's a computer game called "Castles and Quests— Version IV-D." Funny, I don't remember seeing this box before.

VICTOR: Given the dust, it looks like it's been around awhile. Even the box looks kind of old-fashioned, doesn't it?

MR. HILL: It certainly does. But the price looks right! It's marked $14.95, which puts it in your price range. Do you want to take a look at it?

VICTOR: Sure.

Macmillan/McGraw-Hill

NARRATOR: Victor opened the box. There were several computer disks, a little cloth pouch containing some miniature figures, a pencil, some grid paper, a little coil of rope, and a toy flashlight. Underneath everything was a rather tattered-looking instruction booklet. Victor opened the manual and flipped through it.

VICTOR: Hmmm, it looks like a good game. Too bad that some of the pages are missing from the instruction booklet.

MR. HILL: Could be that's the reason I never sold it. Tell you what, Victor. I wouldn't feel right about charging you full price for the game if there's something missing. I could let you have it for half price—if you still want it.

VICTOR: That sounds okay to me. I'm pretty good at figuring out how computer games work. I'll take it.

NARRATOR: Mr. Hill rang up the purchase and wrapped it up.

MR. HILL: So long, Victor. Let me know how the game turns out.

VICTOR: Thanks, Mr. Hill, I will. See you soon.

NARRATOR: When Victor got home, he found his sister Maritza curled up on the window seat watching the raindrops race down the pane.

VICTOR: Hey, Maritza, look what I've got!

MARITZA: Not another computer game! If you ask me, they're all alike.

VICTOR: Well, I didn't ask you! Besides, this is no ordinary computer game—in fact, it might even help me with that social studies project.

MARITZA: Oh, sure. Somehow, I don't think that's quite what Ms. Potter had in mind when she assigned a research project!

VICTOR: Well, I don't see why not. This game is about the Middle Ages. It's called Castles and Quests, and according to the box, it's "designed to help you capture all the excitement of the time."

MARITZA: Sounds like advertising copy to me.

VICTOR: Come on, Maritza, let's just give it a try. It sure beats watching raindrops race on a window!

MARITZA: I suppose you're right. I *am* tired of watching the rain. I'll load the disks while you read the manual.

VICTOR: Uh . . . okay. There is one little thing I forgot to mention, though. You see, Mr. Hill gave me a really good deal on the game because a few of the pages are missing from the booklet. But I'm sure we can figure it out.

MARITZA: Hmmm. . . . The disks have warning labels on them. Listen to this:

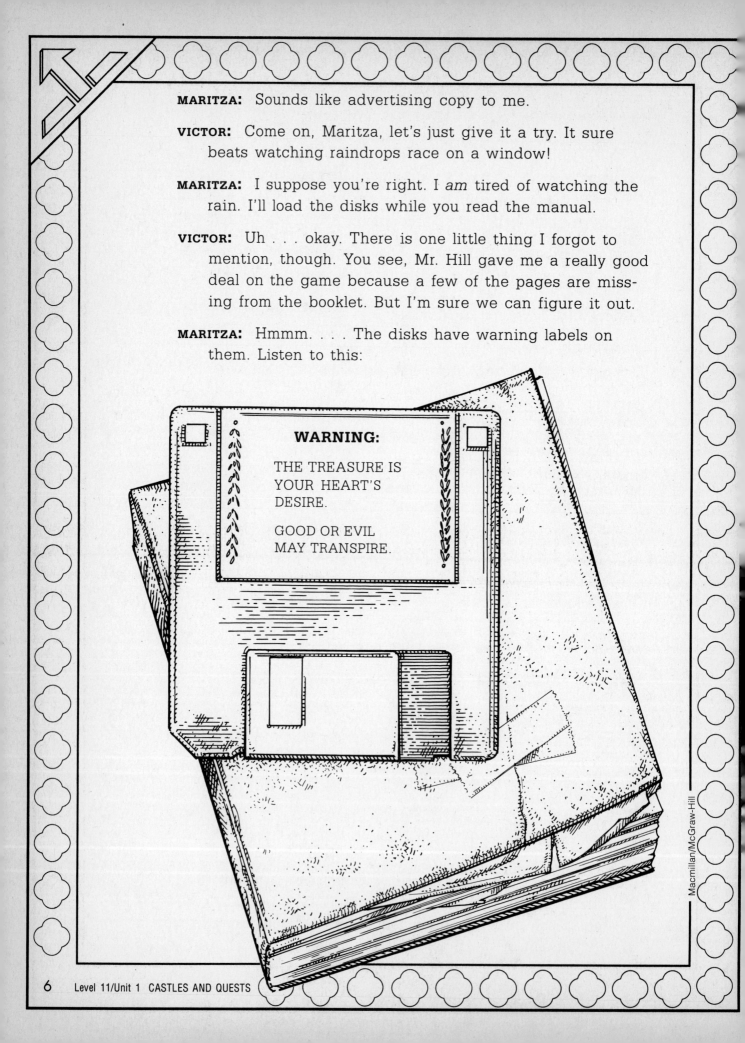

WARNING:

THE TREASURE IS YOUR HEART'S DESIRE.

GOOD OR EVIL MAY TRANSPIRE.

Macmillan/McGraw-Hill

VICTOR: "May transpire?" That doesn't even make sense to me. All I desire right now is to start playing the game. Go ahead and boot the disks.

MARITZA: Okay, here goes. The game has a voice card, so at least the computer can talk to us.

SOUND EFFECT: [*electronic music*]

COMPUTER: Welcome to Castles and Quests. To begin, type [B] and hit <ENTER>.

MARITZA: That's simple enough.

COMPUTER: Working. . . . To create Castles and Quests characters, name each figure in the pouch, describe its powers, and identify it as friend or foe.

MARITZA: Name each figure in the pouch? What does that mean?

NARRATOR: Victor reached into the game box, took out the little bag, and spilled the miniature figures into his hand.

VICTOR: I think this is what the computer is talking about.

MARITZA: Look! There's a knight on the monitor screen who matches one of the miniatures. His armor and shield are made of tiny mirrors.

VICTOR: Let's call this character the Knight of Light. He'll use his shield and armor of mirrors to defeat his foes. The Knight of Light is definitely a friend.

COMPUTER: Working. . . . Knight of Light entered as friend.

MARITZA: Excuse me, Victor, but did you hear that? The computer seemed to understand what you were saying about the knight.

VICTOR: Yeah, that's neat! I guess this voice card works both ways, so that sometimes the computer can process what we're saying without our having to type it in. Let's name the other characters so we can play the game.

NARRATOR: The next character to appear on the screen was a tall woman dressed in long robes. She was carrying a harp. After finding the matching miniature, Maritza named her the Mistress of Song and gave her the power to sing any foe to sleep. Then Victor created one last friend whom he named the Mage of Mirth. This bearded fellow looked like an old-fashioned sorcerer, and Victor gave him the power to cast spells that would send a foe into fits of uncontrollable laughter.

VICTOR: Okay. We've created three friends. The rest of these miniature figures look like foes to me. According to the instruction book, the computer will create characteristics for the foes if we type [F] and hit <ENTER>.

MARITZA: All right. Here goes.

COMPUTER: Working. . . . The first foe is a troll who can turn its victims into enchanted flowers.

VICTOR: Enchanted flowers? This troll is strange.

NARRATOR: In quick succession, the computer also created an orc who could enslave his enemies with irresistible nectar and twin goblins who traveled on a fire-breathing dragon.

MARITZA: I guess that does it; we have our friends and foes. What's next?

VICTOR: The manual says we're supposed to use the grid paper and pencil provided in the box to create a map of the castle and surrounding countryside. Then we use the scanner to enter the map into the computer's memory.

NARRATOR: While Victor sketched the castle, Maritza filled in the surrounding landscape. After passing the scanner over the map, a grassy meadow appeared on the monitor.

MARITZA: Look! That's the meadow I drew. It looks so real, I can almost smell the grass.

VICTOR: It does look real. Now, according to the instructions, we're supposed to put all the miniature figures including the little rope and flashlight back in the pouch and press <ENTER>. Okay, here goes.

COMPUTER: Working. . . . . Version IV-D activating setting.

MARITZA: Now look at the screen. There's the waterfall and the stream I drew. The waterfall seems to be moving off into the distance, almost as if we were walking away from it. Look! Did you see something sparkle to the side of that tree stump?

VICTOR: Yeah . . . it looks like a key to me. The manual says to press [T] if you see an object you want to take. Let's try it.

MARITZA: Victor . . . this is weird. I pressed [T], and all of a sudden, I've got a key in my hand. What's going on?

VICTOR: Don't ask me! Hey . . . I wonder if that's what Version IV-D means?

MARITZA: Huh?

VICTOR: "IV-D"—meaning fourth dimension. Get it?

MARITZA: Victor, you know that waterfall I was just talking about? Well, I hate to tell you this, but it looks like it's materialized on the wall behind the piano, and grass is beginning to sprout from the carpet!

VICTOR: Maritza, I think we'd better quit. Don't you see what this 4-D business is all about? Things from the game are starting to appear in our living room!

MARITZA: Quit? Don't be silly! Look . . . there's a real stream over by the couch. I'm going to get a drink.

Macmillan/McGraw-Hill

VICTOR: Get a drink? You've got to be kidding! Don't eat or drink anything, or who knows what will happen! This game is definitely out of control.

MARITZA: Okay, okay, I won't, but come over here and take a look. There's another gold key caught between some rocks in the stream. I'm going to add it to our key collection.

VICTOR: Maritza, I've had enough of Castles and Quests. We've got to get this stream out of the living room. Now get out of there, dry off, and help me turn this game off!

NARRATOR: Maritza stepped out of the stream and put the two keys into the pouch with the other miniatures. Then she began flipping through the instruction book looking for the sign-off procedures.

MARITZA: Victor, here's something else I hate to tell you— you know the pages that tell you how to exit from the game? Well, they're missing from the manual!

VICTOR: Oh, great! Well, we'll just have to try out different combinations and hope that one works.

NARRATOR: Victor and Maritza began pressing keys wildly, trying to figure out how to stop the game. With each attempt, another piece of living-room furniture was transformed into a boulder or a tree. Soon the walls began to fade, and off in the distance, the two could see a forest of tall trees. As their surroundings changed, something remarkable happened to Victor and Maritza, too.

VICTOR: Maritza . . . look at you! You look exactly as if you lived in the Middle Ages.

MARITZA: You, too. You look just like that picture of a squire in our social studies book!

NARRATOR: Maritza and Victor were so busy inspecting their new clothing that they failed to hear the sound of footsteps.

SOUND EFFECT: [approaching footsteps]

KNIGHT: Halt! Who goes there? Friend or foe?

VICTOR: Maritza, look! It's the Knight of Light! Why, we're definitely friends, Sir Knight.

KNIGHT: I trust thou speakest the truth. Come out, Mistress of Song and Mage of Mirth. All appears to be safe.

MARITZA: Victor, do you get it? Those are the characters we created with the computer. We're really part of the game!

VICTOR: Right, but if the friends we created are part of the game, then the foes that the computer created must be lurking around somewhere.

SONG MISTRESS: Foes? You are right, young sir. Foes there are aplenty, and they are in search of us!

MARITZA: Really? Why is that?

MAGE OF MIRTH: Because of this, fair maid!

NARRATOR: With that, the Mage of Mirth reached into a large pouch and pulled out a tattered half of a map.

VICTOR: What's that?

KNIGHT: Why, 'tis part of a treasure map. You see, we three companions are on a quest in search of the treasure. We must hasten to reach it before the foes find it; otherwise, calamity will result!

VICTOR: Calamity will result? What do you mean?

MAGE OF MIRTH: The treasure is your heart's desire. If the finder is a friend, the treasure will work for good. If the finder is a foe, the treasure will work for evil.

MARITZA: So that's what the warning on the disks meant!

VICTOR: Could I see that map for a minute? It looks strangely familiar.

MARITZA: Of course, it does. We've got the other half!

MAGE/KNIGHT/SONG MISTRESS: You do?

VICTOR: We do? Where?

MARITZA: In the back of the instruction book, silly. Look, the pieces match perfectly.

Macmillan/McGraw-Hill

NARRATOR: As everyone watched, Maritza carefully put the two pieces side by side. Suddenly, with a blinding flash of light, the two sides fused! The map continued to glow for an instant and then faded.

KNIGHT: You are friends, indeed. Now we must hasten to find the treasure before the foes reach it.

SONG MISTRESS: Our path leads directly through the dark forest and into the goblins' castle. This is not a journey for the faint of heart.

MARITZA: I've never fainted in my life, even when I got a black eye from a wild pitch! Lead on, Sir Knight of Light.

VICTOR: Light . . . that reminds me, we've got a flashlight. Look!

NARRATOR: With that, Victor reached into the game pouch and pulled out the tiny light. It began to glow with a faint blue light as it slowly grew to full size.

MAGE OF MIRTH: Zounds! A torch that burneth without fire! A most worthy display of talent, lad.

KNIGHT: Shine the torch upon my armor. You can follow its light as it reflects off me.

NARRATOR: Without a backward glance, the band plunged into the forest, careful to stay within the narrow corridor of light created by the knight's shining armor. Soon, the tall towers of a bleak-looking castle loomed ahead.

VICTOR: Oh, if only Ms. Potter could see this castle! It looks so real.

SONG MISTRESS: Ms. Potter? I know not the name! This castle belongs to the goblin twins.

MAGE OF MIRTH: The treasure that we seek lies within. But first we must find a way past the troll who guards the flower-filled moat.

VICTOR: Uh-oh, Maritza, remember the troll?

MARITZA: Yeah, how could I forget? The computer gave it the power to turn its enemies into flowers. Why, all those flowers must be the troll's victims!

KNIGHT: Lad and maid, hide thee behind me! Behold, the troll rises from its murky lair to block our entrance to the castle.

TROLL: And who will be first to join my floating garden? Old Mage, which suits you best, a rose or a tulip?

SONG MISTRESS: Ladies first, kind troll. And as you weave your spell, allow me to entertain you with my melody!

NARRATOR: Without delay, the Mistress of Song began to sing and play a beautiful melody upon her harp.

TROLL: Sing, if you will, for your voice is pleasant enough. Hold. What trickery is this? . . . My eyelids grow heavy! I fall asleep!

SOUND EFFECT: [*splash*]

NARRATOR: With a tremendous splash, the troll tumbled off the drawbridge into the moat!

MAGE OF MIRTH: The troll is now a weed that floateth among the flowers! Good work, indeed, Mistress of Song.

SONG MISTRESS: Thank you, kind Mage. I do regret the energy that took; I will not be able to repeat that feat again for days.

MARITZA: If we're lucky, we won't run into any more foes. According to the map, we must enter the castle through a side gate, turn left, and follow a passageway until we reach a door.

KNIGHT: Stay together and follow me!

MAGE OF MIRTH: I liketh not this passageway. There are no signs of life along these cold stone walls. Where are the spiders and scorpions? Where are the mice and the scurrying rats?

VICTOR: You've got to be kidding! . . . Just wait until Mr. Hill hears about this! Nothing on the game box mentioned anything about scorpions and rats!

MARITZA: Maybe that's what was meant by "capturing the excitement of the time!"

SONG MISTRESS: Look yonder! I see a heavy oaken door at the end of the passageway.

KNIGHT: Stand back whilst I open it. . . . 'Twill not budge. The door is held fast, as if by magic spell.

MARITZA: Shh! Everybody quiet. . . . Do you hear a rushing sound?

SOUND EFFECT: [rushing water]

MAGE OF MIRTH: 'Tis undoubtedly the wind that fills the corridor.

VICTOR: That's not wind—it's water! I can feel it seeping through my shoes! The passageway is filling with water!

SONG MISTRESS: It's a trap! Make haste! We must try the door yet again. Everyone, push with all your might!

MAGE OF MIRTH: 'Tis no use. This door is held fast by enchantment. If only thou had given me a spell to unfasten bolts firmly held in place. A spell such as that would have been the key.

Macmillan/McGraw-Hill

MARITZA: Key? Did you say key? Victor, remember the two keys I found? Quick, where are they? Maybe one of them will fit.

SONG MISTRESS: Make haste! The water has reached my knees and is rising quickly.

VICTOR: Here they are, Maritza. I'll try the big one first. . . . No! It's much too large.

SOUND EFFECT: [*jingle of keys*]

KNIGHT: The other one, lad. Try the other one!

NARRATOR: Victor fished the other key out of the pouch and slipped it into the lock.

MARITZA: It fits! It fits! Everyone, push!

SOUND EFFECT: [*creaking door*]

NARRATOR: The massive door slowly pivoted on its rusty hinges, and the group slipped through and shut the door behind them on the rising flood.

VICTOR: Wow! I call that too close for comfort!

KNIGHT: Do not rejoice too soon, lad. Untold dangers still lurk within these castle walls.

MAGE OF MIRTH: Truly spoken, Sir Knight. Look around you! We are held fast within a prison chamber. We cannot exit the way we entered, for the rising tide will surely drown us. And here the windows and remaining door are secured with heavy iron bars and lengths of chain! Methinks we are trapped anew.

SONG MISTRESS: The other key, young maiden! Try the one that was too large for the door.

MARITZA: Right . . . the large key. . . . Victor, quick! Check the pouch! Is it still there?

VICTOR: It should be. Hold on. . . . Now where did I put it?

KNIGHT: Hark, I hear approaching footsteps. Make haste!

SOUND EFFECT: [*approaching footsteps*]

VICTOR: Here it is! Quick, does it fit?

MARITZA: Not a chance. It's not the right shape.

MAGE OF MIRTH: Behold, our jailer cometh!

VICTOR: Why, it's an orc that looks exactly like the miniature in the game pouch!

MARITZA: Yeah, the only visible difference is a slight change in height—like about six feet! What's he carrying?

VICTOR: It looks like a tray with bowls full of liquid to me!

MAGE OF MIRTH: Beware of orcs bearing gifts! The nectar in those bowls is laced with enchantment.

MARITZA: Enchanted or not, I'm starving. Besides, it smells like my favorite food—won ton soup!

KNIGHT: Wrong, fair maiden. I detect the succulent aroma of roast pig.

SONG MISTRESS: Thou art in error, Sir Knight! The sweet scent of candied violets is what you smell.

VICTOR: You're all wrong. How could anybody mistake the delicious smell of barbecued ribs?

ORC: That's right! You're all right! Eat! Eat! And then eat some more. There's plenty more where this came from.

MAGE OF MIRTH: Beware, taste not this orc's nectar! One drop will hold thee tighter than twenty chains and locks. Canst thou not see through this fiendish orc's trickery?

ORC: Clever Mage, you are right. My nectar does have a taste that holds one fast, but none are able to resist! So eat and be merry—for all eternity! Ha, ha, ha!

MAGE OF MIRTH: Thy laughter remindeth me of a spell—a spell to repay the kindness thou hast shown us. Stand well back, everyone: CHUCKLE! CHORTLE! CACKLE! GUFFAW!

NARRATOR: Bright blue flames shot out from the long fingers of the mage. There was a sudden crash and clatter as the orc dropped his loaded tray.

SOUND EFFECT: [*falling dishes*]

ORC: Ha, ha ha! . . . Ho, ho, ho! . . . Hee, hee, hee!

MARITZA: The laughing spell! Remember, Victor? We gave the mage the power to send a foe into a fit of uncontrollable laughter.

VICTOR: Well, it certainly did the trick! Good work, Mage of Mirth.

MAGE OF MIRTH: Thank you, my lad. Now, verily, we must escape before the spell is exhausted and the orc regains his composure.

KNIGHT: This foolish orc hath left the cell door open! Make haste and follow me!

MARITZA: According to the map, we continue down the corridor until we reach a stairway on the left. It's a shortcut that leads directly to the dungeon where the treasure is buried.

VICTOR: Great, but how are we ever going to get home?

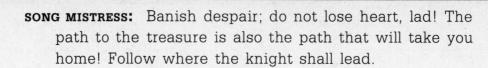

SONG MISTRESS: Banish despair; do not lose heart, lad! The path to the treasure is also the path that will take you home! Follow where the knight shall lead.

VICTOR: Did you hear that, Maritza? Lead on, Sir Knight.

NARRATOR: The group followed the knight on and on, through the winding corridor until, finally, they reached the door on the left. It swung open easily, and the knight led them through.

SOUND EFFECT: [*heavy door shutting with a clang*]

MAGE OF MIRTH: Well, 'tis too late to turn back now, for the door is shut fast behind us. Let us hope we are on the right path.

SONG MISTRESS: Halt! I can feel the stones shifting beneath my feet! Quick! Move back!

Macmillan/McGraw-Hill

NARRATOR: Seconds later, a huge slab set in the stone floor tilted forward, and a gaping pit opened up at their feet!

VICTOR: One more step and we'd have been goners!

MARITZA: Yeah! If that's a short cut to the nearest dungeon, I think I'd rather take the long way around!

KNIGHT: There is a sturdy beam above the pit. If only I had brought the length of rope that is tied to my saddle.

VICTOR: Rope? Did you say *rope*? Why, there's a tiny coil of rope in the game pouch. Just a minute, and I'll see if I can find it. . . . Here it is!

NARRATOR: Victor held out his hand with the toy coil of rope. When the knight took it, there was a sudden flash of light as the rope was transformed.

MARITZA: Look, it's become real!

KNIGHT: Thanks, good lad. Now I must toss the rope o'er the beam so we may swing across the pit. Arm, fail me not.

NARRATOR: With a mighty heave, the knight hurled the rope over the beam and tied the ends together to make a rope seat. Each member of the group, in turn, swung across the bottomless pit and safely reached the other side. Following the map, they descended the steep steps into the rank-smelling dungeon.

MAGE OF MIRTH: We must hurry! My ring has turned blue—a sign that goblins lurk nearby.

SONG MISTRESS: Your warning comes too late, wise Mage, for I see the goblins up ahead perched on the back of their pet dragon.

MARITZA: Some pet! Look at the flames coming out of its mouth!

DRAGON: You trespass-s-s-s. S-s-s-stand back!

GOBLIN 1: We see you've crossed the bottomless pit!

GOBLIN 2: But to get past us will take more wit!

GOBLIN 1: Seeing you roast will be our pleasure!

GOBLIN 2: We'll take the map and claim the treasure!

KNIGHT: We must advance; there is no turning back!

MAGE OF MIRTH: But how? Both the Mistress of Song and I have exhausted our powers defeating the troll and the orc. We can do nothing against the goblins and their loathsome dragon.

MARITZA: Does this mean that we'll be trapped in this game forever?

VICTOR: Maritza and I *really* do need to get home. I've got a social studies project that's due in a week, and I've barely started!

MARITZA: Victor, excuse me for saying this, but at this moment, I would say that your social studies project is the least of our worries!

GOBLIN 1: Now hand over the map, and we'll be nice!

GOBLIN 2: If you choose otherwise, you'll pay the price!

GOBLIN 1: Our dragon's burner is set on high!

GOBLIN 2: So give us the map or you will . . .

MAGE OF MIRTH: Cease! Or I will end your rhymes with a fit of laughter.

DRAGON: S-s-s-silence, S-s-s-sorceror!

GOBLIN 1: You don't frighten us, O Mage of Mirth!

GOBLIN 2: Your powers are of little worth!

GOBLIN 1: You spent them all on the orc, we know!

GOBLIN 2: Now dragon's breath, begin to glow!

DRAGON: Yes-s-s-s, Masters-s-s-s!

NARRATOR: With that, a tongue of flame shot out of the dragon's mouth and hit the hem of the mage's cloak.

MARITZA: Mage! Your cloak is on fire!

SONG MISTRESS: Quick, lad; help me stamp it out!

Macmillan/McGraw-Hill

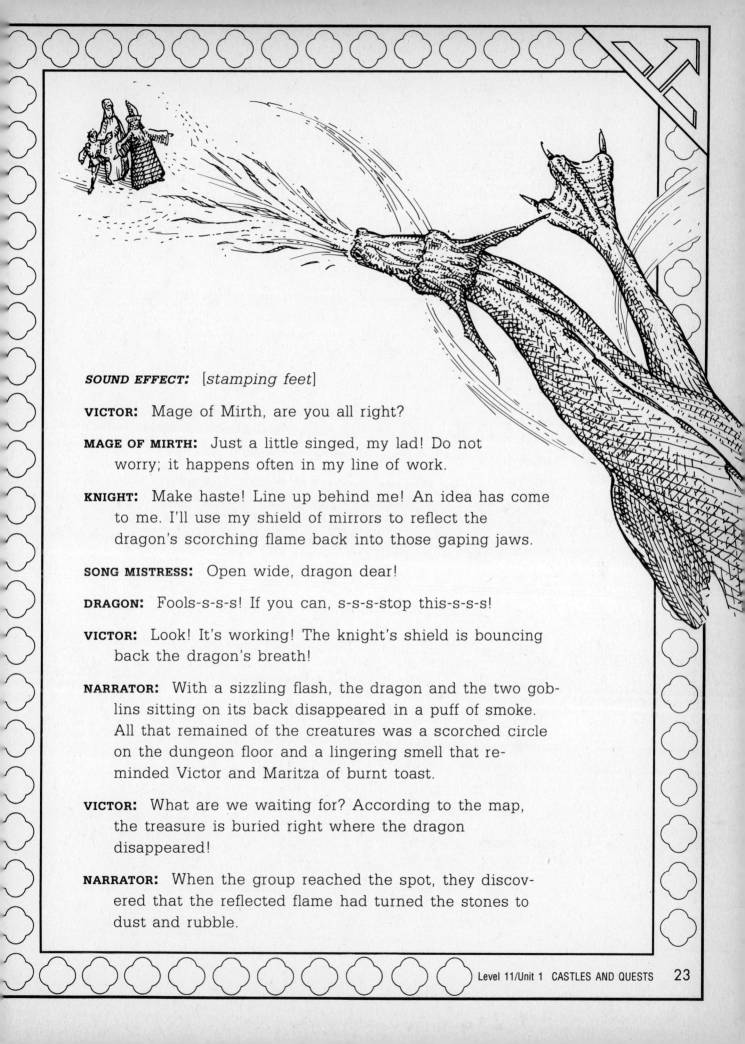

SOUND EFFECT: [*stamping feet*]

VICTOR: Mage of Mirth, are you all right?

MAGE OF MIRTH: Just a little singed, my lad! Do not worry; it happens often in my line of work.

KNIGHT: Make haste! Line up behind me! An idea has come to me. I'll use my shield of mirrors to reflect the dragon's scorching flame back into those gaping jaws.

SONG MISTRESS: Open wide, dragon dear!

DRAGON: Fools-s-s-s! If you can, s-s-s-stop this-s-s-s!

VICTOR: Look! It's working! The knight's shield is bouncing back the dragon's breath!

NARRATOR: With a sizzling flash, the dragon and the two goblins sitting on its back disappeared in a puff of smoke. All that remained of the creatures was a scorched circle on the dungeon floor and a lingering smell that reminded Victor and Maritza of burnt toast.

VICTOR: What are we waiting for? According to the map, the treasure is buried right where the dragon disappeared!

NARRATOR: When the group reached the spot, they discovered that the reflected flame had turned the stones to dust and rubble.

MAGE OF MIRTH: Look sharp! My eyes detect the glint of gold.

VICTOR: You're right, Mage. It looks like the corner of a golden chest.

SONG MISTRESS: That, young sir, is the treasure casket! We have reached the end of our quest. The treasure has been found!

MARITZA: Well, we may have found the treasure, but I don't see how that will help us get home.

KNIGHT: Open the treasure casket, fair maiden, for thou hast the key.

VICTOR: Maritza, try the other key . . . you know, the one that wouldn't fit in the cell door.

NARRATOR: Maritza carefully inserted the key in the lock. With a click, the lid flew open, and everyone crowded around to peer in.

MARITZA: Look, everybody! It's our house. That's the living room and the computer where this game started.

VICTOR: That's our house, all right! Mage, can you tell us how we can get back to where we belong?

MAGE OF MIRTH: Remember: "The treasure is your heart's desire." All you must do is wish for what you see in the treasure casket.

MARITZA: You've all been so kind. Won't you come back with us?

VICTOR: Please do! I'd really like you to meet Mr. Hill!

MARITZA: How about introducing them to Ms. Potter? I'm positive she'd give you extra credit for bringing a mage, a fair lady, and a knight in full armor into school as guest speakers!

SONG MISTRESS: Thank you for your kind invitation, young sir and fair maid. We must remain here, for our world is the land of Castles and Quests. But we trust that you will visit us anon.

VICTOR: Oh, yes! I promise that we'll be back . . . right after I get my social studies report done!

NARRATOR: After exchanging warm farewells, Victor and Maritza picked up the treasure casket, and holding it between them, wished with all their might.

MARITZA/VICTOR: Home is my heart's desire!

NARRATOR: With that, the walls of the dungeon began to fade. Behind the stones, the walls of the living room gradually began to reappear.

MARITZA: Look, Victor! We're home, and everything looks just like it did before we started playing the game! Hey! Where are you going?

VICTOR: I'm going back to Mr. Hill's toy store before it closes.

MARITZA: How come? You're not going to return Castles and Quests, are you?

VICTOR: Are you kidding? I want to check out another box in Mr. Hill's shop that looked just like this one.

MARITZA: Excuse me?

VICTOR: Yeah . . . it was called Pyramids and Pursuits!

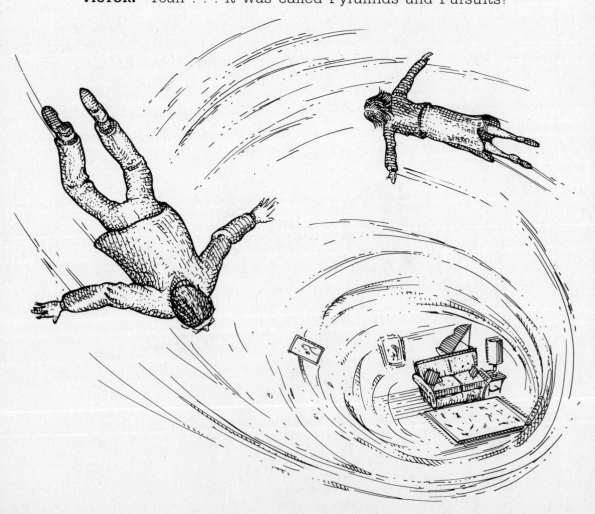

Macmillan/McGraw-Hill

BLOCKING DIAGRAM

Arrange eight chairs, a stool, and a bench, as shown.
The narrator can use a music stand to hold the script.

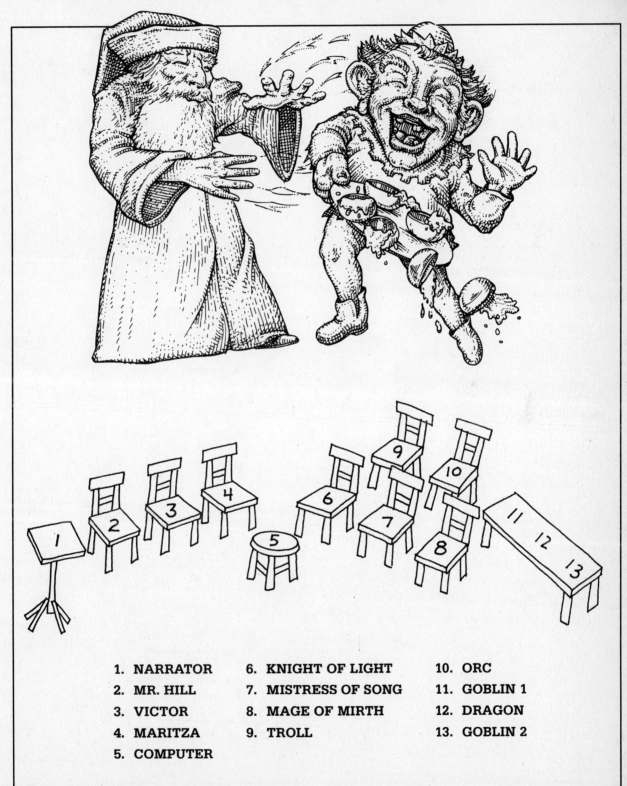

1. NARRATOR
2. MR. HILL
3. VICTOR
4. MARITZA
5. COMPUTER

6. KNIGHT OF LIGHT
7. MISTRESS OF SONG
8. MAGE OF MIRTH
9. TROLL

10. ORC
11. GOBLIN 1
12. DRAGON
13. GOBLIN 2

PUPPETS

MISTRESS
OF SONG

KNIGHT OF LIGHT

MAGE OF MIRTH

GOBLIN

DRAGON

ORC

TROLL

General Directions for Assembling Puppets

Step One: Assemble all materials.

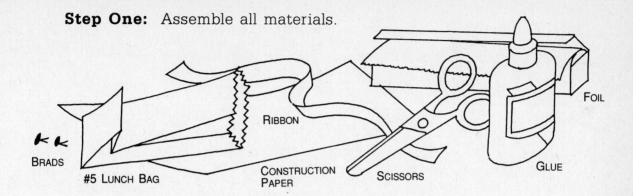

BRADS

#5 LUNCH BAG

RIBBON

CONSTRUCTION PAPER

SCISSORS

GLUE

FOIL

Step Two: Prepare the bag.

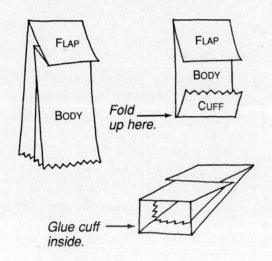

FLAP

BODY

FLAP

BODY

CUFF

Fold up here.

Glue cuff inside.

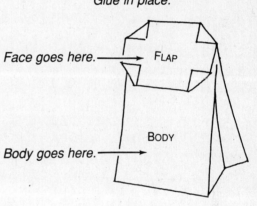

Fold down corners of the bag. Glue in place.

Face goes here. → FLAP

Body goes here. → BODY

Step Three: Cut out the pattern pieces.

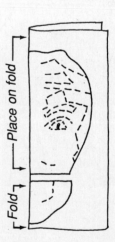

Place on fold

Fold

Cut a single piece.

(× 2)

The symbol (x2) means cut two of this piece. Flip the pattern over when cutting the second piece.

Place the fold line of the pattern on folded construction paper. Then cut.

Step Four: Transfer pattern to the puppet pieces.

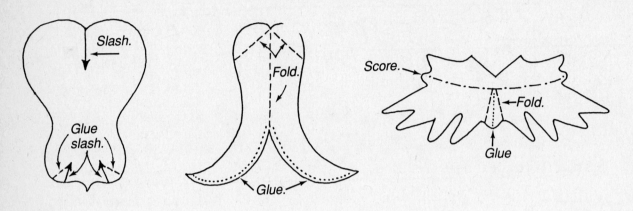

slash lines

fold and glue lines

score lines (To score, run the dull side of a scissors along the score line; this dents the paper.)

Step Five: Shape the jaws. (This applies to Dragon, Orc, Troll, and Goblin.)

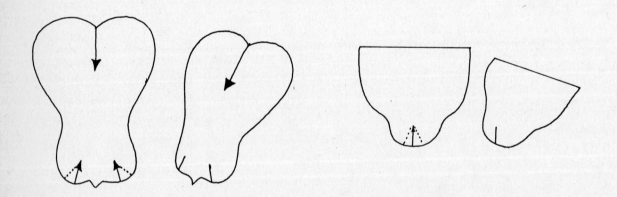

(Slit on solid lines; put glue in the triangle next to slit. Overlap slit edge to dotted line and press.)

(Cut the center slit; put glue in each triangle and press the sides together.)

Step Six: Glue the body parts to the bag.

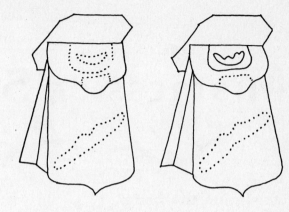

Glue arms under chest.

Glue chest on the body part of bag; glue lower jaw on chest; glue teeth and inner mouth on the lower jaw; glue jewelry to chest. (See individual directions for specific gluing order.)

Step Seven: Glue the face to the bag.

Put glue on the dotted lines; round the nose over a pencil while attaching it to the head.

Glue all the head parts on the bag flap. (See individual puppet directions for specific gluing order.)

Directions for Assembling Individual Puppets

MISTRESS OF SONG

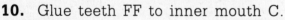

Assemble the body.

1. Glue chest O to body of bag.
2. Glue neckline T to chest O.
3. Glue jewelry QQ to chest O around neckline T.
4. Score each section of cape OO.
5. Glue cape sections OO to each side of chest O.
6. Fold the outside edge of cape OO back along the scored line.
7. Glue jewelry QQ1 to chest O and jewelry QQ.
8. Glue lower jaw B to chest O on top of neckline T. (Put glue on only one inch at the top of the underside of the jaw.)
9. Glue inner mouth C to lower jaw B and the underside of the bag flap.
10. Glue teeth FF to inner mouth C.

Macmillan/McGraw-Hill

Assemble the head.

1. Glue head A to the bag flap. (Make sure the straight edge at the base of head A is glued along the straight edge at the bottom of the bag flap.)
2. Glue nose D to head A.
3. Glue lips E to head A.
4. Assemble eyes:
   a. Glue irises GG to eyewhites G.
   b. Glue pupils H to irises GG.
5. Glue assembled eyes to head A.
6. Glue eyelids HH over eyes to head A.
7. Glue eyebrows I over eyelids HH to head A.
8. Glue hair L to head A.
9. Glue crown R to hair L.

MISTRESS OF SONG PATTERN

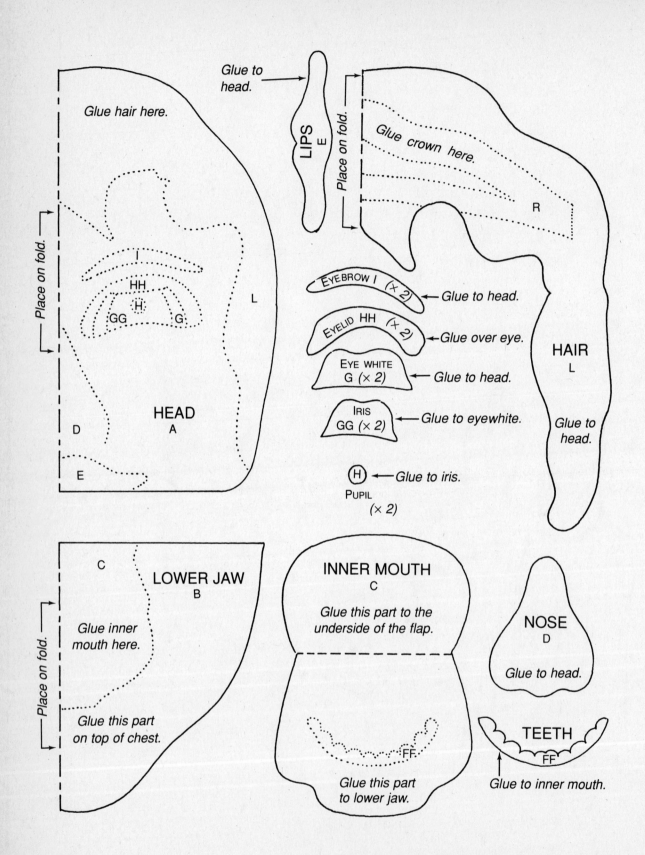

Glue to head.

LIPS
E

Place on fold.

Glue crown here.

Glue hair here.

Place on fold.

I

HH

H

GG   G

L

HEAD
A

D

E

EYEBROW I (×2) ← Glue to head.

EYELID HH (×2) ← Glue over eye.

EYE WHITE
G (×2) ← Glue to head.

IRIS
GG (×2) ← Glue to eyewhite.

H ← Glue to iris.
PUPIL
(×2)

R

HAIR
L

Glue to head.

C

LOWER JAW
B

Glue inner
mouth here.

Place on fold.

Glue this part
on top of chest.

INNER MOUTH
C

Glue this part to the
underside of the flap.

FF

Glue this part
to lower jaw.

NOSE
D

Glue to head.

TEETH
FF

Glue to inner mouth.

MISTRESS OF SONG PATTERN

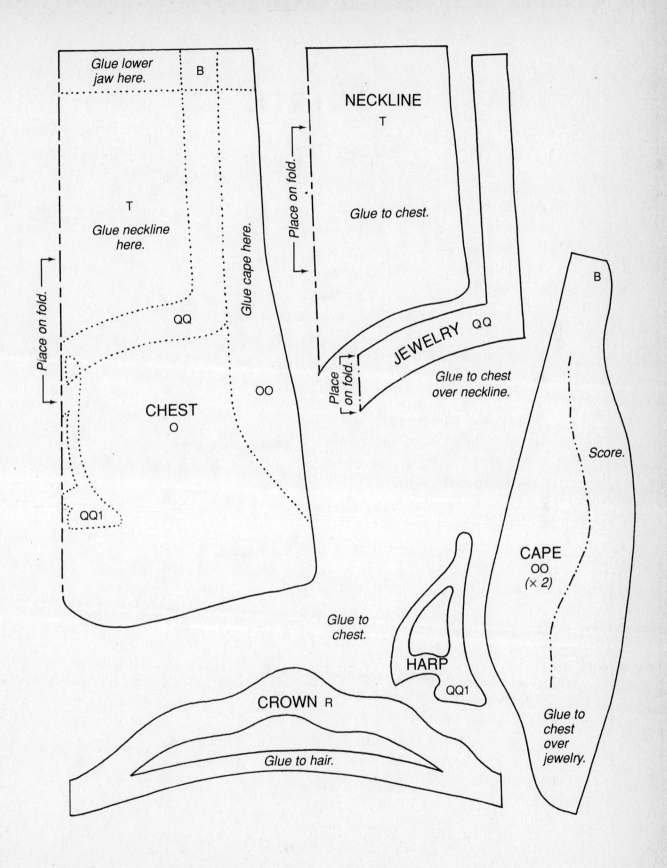

Mage of Mirth

Assemble the body.

1. Glue chest O to body of bag.
2. Glue jewelry QQ to chest O.
3. Glue jewelry QQ1 to jewelry QQ.
4. Glue lower jaw B to chest O. (Put glue on only one inch at the top of the underside of the jaw.)
5. Glue inner mouth C to lower jaw B.
6. Glue teeth FF to inner mouth C.
7. Glue beard KK to lower jaw B.

Assemble the head.

1. Glue head A to the bag flap. (Make sure the straight edge at the base of head A is glued along the straight edge at the bottom of the bag flap.)
2. Glue nose D to head A.
3. Glue lips E to head A.
4. Glue moustache II above lips E to head A.
5. Assemble eyes:
   a. Glue irises GG to eyewhites G.
   b. Glue pupils H to irises GG.
6. Glue assembled eyes to head A.
7. Glue eyelids HH over eyes to head A.
8. Glue eyebrows I over eyelids HH to head A.
9. Glue hair L to head A.
10. Fold up brim of hat R.
11. Glue the hat R to hair L (do not glue down the folded brim).
12. Glue hat trims SS and SS1 to hat R.

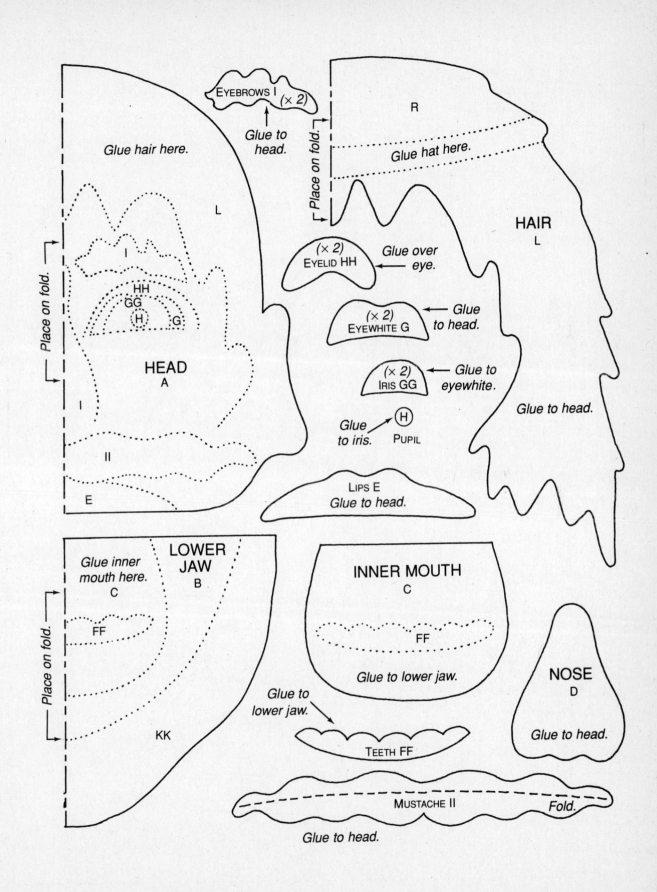

EYEBROWS I (×2)
Glue to head.

Glue hair here.

Place on fold.

R

Glue hat here.

HAIR
L

L

I

(×2)
EYELID HH
Glue over eye.

HH
GG
(H) G

(×2)
EYEWHITE G
Glue to head.

HEAD
A

(×2)
IRIS GG
Glue to eyewhite.

I

Glue to head.

Glue to iris. (H) PUPIL

II

E

LIPS E
Glue to head.

LOWER JAW
B

Glue inner mouth here.
C

INNER MOUTH
C

Place on fold.

FF

FF

Glue to lower jaw.

NOSE
D

Glue to lower jaw.

Glue to head.

KK

TEETH FF

MUSTACHE II   Fold.

Glue to head.

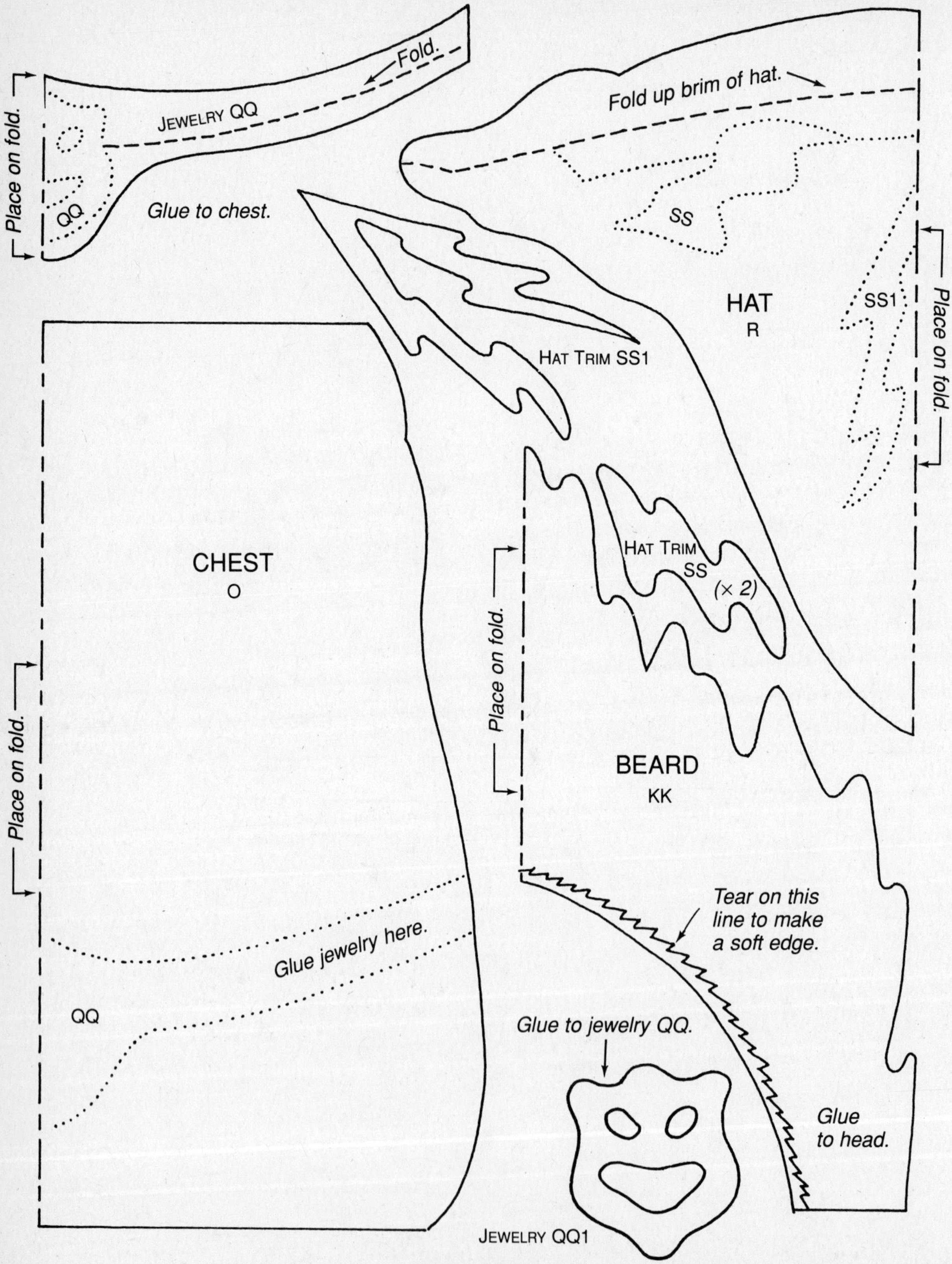

MAGE OF MIRTH PATTERN

JEWELRY QQ

Fold.

Place on fold.

QQ

Glue to chest.

Fold up brim of hat.

SS

HAT
R

SS1

Place on fold.

HAT TRIM SS1

CHEST
O

HAT TRIM
SS *(× 2)*

Place on fold.

Place on fold.

BEARD
KK

Tear on this line to make a soft edge.

QQ

Glue jewelry here.

Glue to jewelry QQ.

Glue to head.

JEWELRY QQ1

Macmillan/McGraw-Hill

KNIGHT OF LIGHT

Assemble the body.

1. Glue chest O to body of bag.
2. Glue jewelry QQ to chest O.
3. Glue lower jaw B to chest O. (Put glue on only one inch at the top of the underside of the jaw.)
4. Glue inner mouth C to lower jaw B.
5. Glue teeth FF to inner mouth C.
6. Glue beard KK to lower jaw B.

Assemble the head.

1. Glue head A to the bag flap. (Make sure the straight edge at the base of head A is glued along the straight edge at the bottom of the bag flap.)
2. Glue nose D to head A.
3. Glue lips E to head A.
4. Glue moustache II above lips E to head A.
5. Assemble eyes:
   a. Glue irises GG to eyewhites G.
   b. Glue pupils H to irises GG.
6. Glue assembled eyes to head A.
7. Glue eyelids HH over eyes to head A.
8. Glue hair L to head A.
9. Score eyebrows I and fold the top part down a little.
10. Glue bottom part of eyebrows I over eyelids HH on head A. (The eyebrows will cover part of hair L.)
11. Assemble helmet R:
    a. Glue plume SS to helmet R.
    b. Glue helmet band SS1 over plume SS on helmet R.
    c. Punch holes in the tops of ears on head A.
    d. Punch holes in each side of helmet R.
    e. Push brads through the holes on each side of the helmet R and through the holes in the tops of the ears on head A.
    f. Spread the brads on the back of head A; the helmet R will stand out from the head.

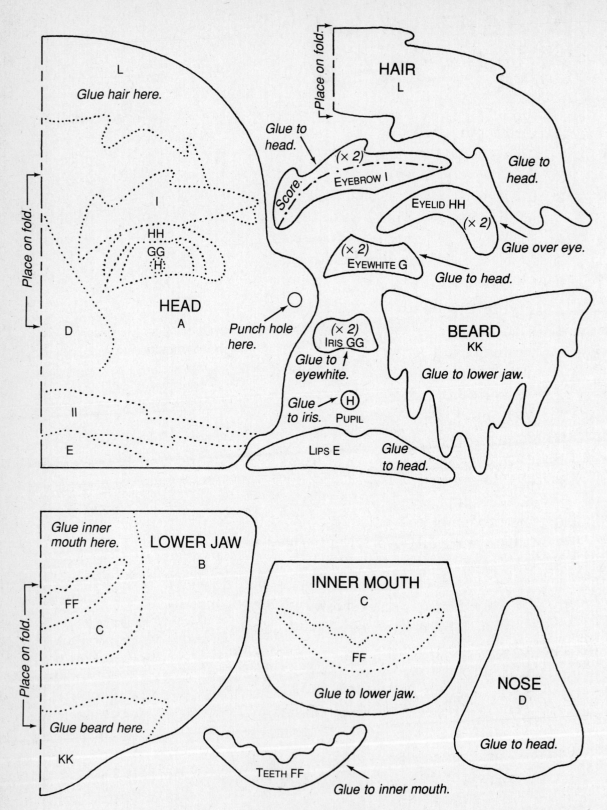

Glue hair here.

L

Place on fold.

I

HH
GG
H

HEAD
A

D

Punch hole here.

II

E

Place on fold.

HAIR
L

Glue to head.

Glue to head.

Score.

(× 2)
EYEBROW I

EYELID HH
(× 2)

Glue over eye.

(× 2)
EYEWHITE G

Glue to head.

(× 2)
IRIS GG

Glue to eyewhite.

Glue to iris.

H
PUPIL

BEARD
KK

Glue to lower jaw.

LIPS E

Glue to head.

Glue inner mouth here.

LOWER JAW
B

FF

C

Glue beard here.

KK

Place on fold.

INNER MOUTH
C

FF

Glue to lower jaw.

TEETH FF

Glue to inner mouth.

NOSE
D

Glue to head.

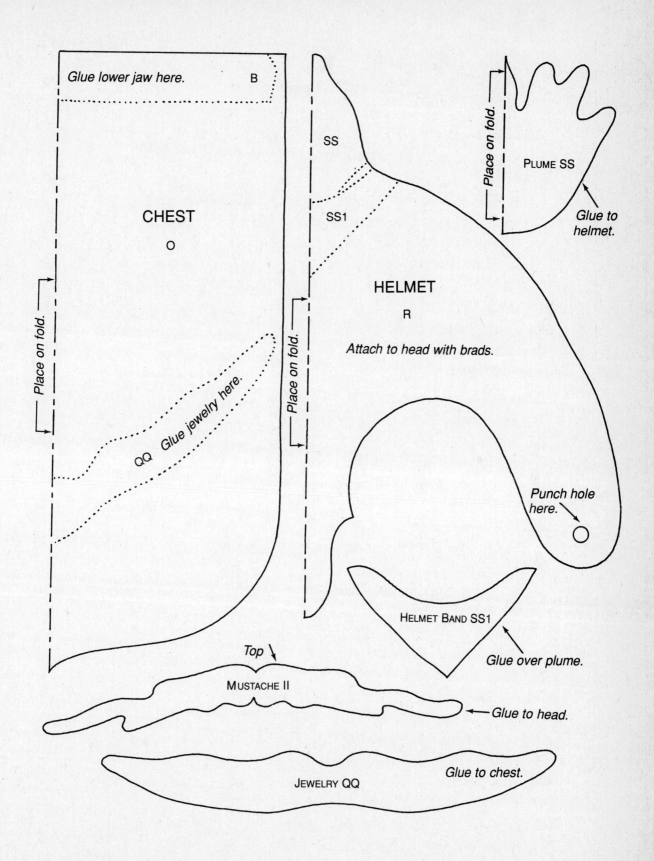

Glue lower jaw here.   B

CHEST

O

Place on fold.

QQ   Glue jewelry here.

SS

SS1

HELMET

R

Attach to head with brads.

Place on fold.

Place on fold.

PLUME SS

Glue to helmet.

Punch hole here.

HELMET BAND SS1

Glue over plume.

Top

MUSTACHE II

Glue to head.

JEWELRY QQ

Glue to chest.

ORC

Assemble the body.

1. Glue chest O to body of bag.
2. Form lower jaw B:
   a. Cut a 1/2 inch slit at center bottom of lower jaw B.
   b. Put glue on each side of the slit in a triangle shape and press the sides together.
   c. Turn the jaw so the curved part of lower jaw B faces chest O.
3. Glue lower jaw B to chest O. (Put glue on only one inch at the top of the underside of the jaw.)
4. Fold inner mouth C so it curves down a little.
5. Glue inner mouth C to lower jaw B.
6. Fold teeth. Glue teeth FF to inner mouth C.

Assemble the head.

1. Glue head A to the bag flap.
2. Form nose D:
   a. Score and fold down. Cut each slit.
   b. Put glue in both triangles on bottom of nose D. Overlap the slit edge to the dotted line and press.
3. Glue nose D to head A.
4. Score lips E and glue top part to head A.
5. Form ears N:
   a. Score and cut a slit.
   b. Put glue in the triangle next to the slit. Overlap the slit edge to the dotted line and press.
6. Glue ears N to head A.
7. Assemble eyes:
   a. Glue irises GG to eyewhites G.
   b. Glue pupils H to eyewhites G.
8. Glue assembled eyes to head A.
9. Fold eyelids HH and glue over eye to head A.
10. Fold eyebrows I and glue over top of eyelids HH to head A.
11. Fold head bump MM and glue to head A.
12. Score hair L. Fold and glue hair L on the center fold lines.
13. Glue hair L over head bump MM to head A.

Macmillan/McGraw-Hill

ORC PATTERN

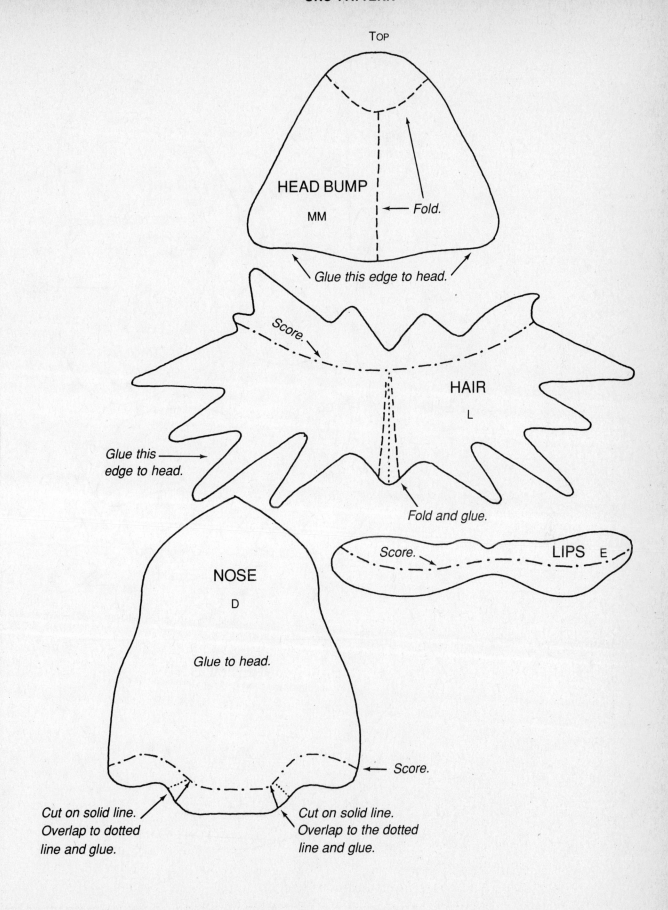

TOP

HEAD BUMP

MM

Fold.

Glue this edge to head.

Score.

HAIR

L

Glue this edge to head.

Fold and glue.

Score. **LIPS** E

NOSE

D

Glue to head.

Score.

Cut on solid line. Overlap to dotted line and glue.

Cut on solid line. Overlap to the dotted line and glue.

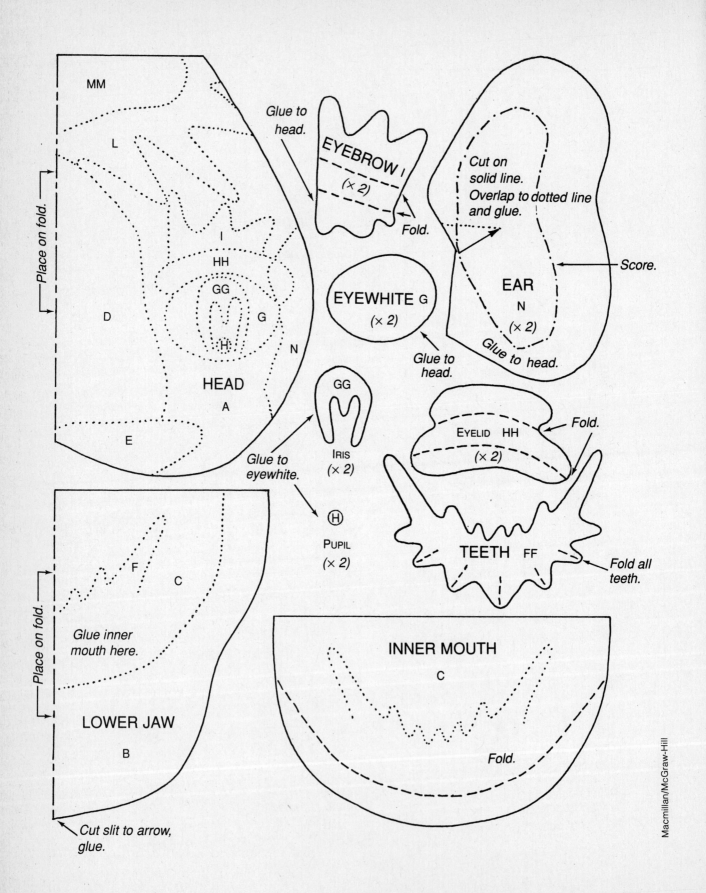

MM

Glue to head.

EYEBROW I

(× 2)

Fold.

L

Place on fold.

I

HH

GG

D

G

H

N

HEAD

A

E

Cut on
solid line.
Overlap to dotted line
and glue.

Score.

EYEWHITE G

(× 2)

EAR

N

(× 2)

Glue to head.

Glue to head.

GG

*Glue to
eyewhite.*

IRIS

(× 2)

Ⓗ

PUPIL

(× 2)

EYELID HH

(× 2)

Fold.

TEETH FF

*Fold all
teeth.*

F

C

*Glue inner
mouth here.*

INNER MOUTH

C

Place on fold.

LOWER JAW

B

Fold.

*Cut slit to arrow,
glue.*

Macmillan/McGraw-Hill

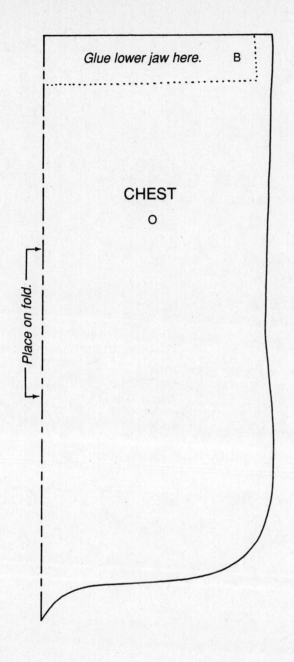

Glue lower jaw here. B

CHEST

o

Place on fold.

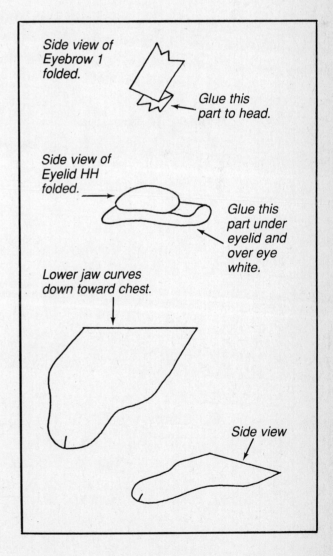

Side view of
Eyebrow 1
folded.

Glue this
part to head.

Side view of
Eyelid HH
folded.

Glue this
part under
eyelid and
over eye
white.

Lower jaw curves
down toward chest.

Side view

TROLL

Assemble the body.

1. Glue chest O to body of bag.
2. Glue chest plate T to chest O. (Put glue on only one inch at the top of the underside of the chest plate.)
3. Form lower jaw B:
   a. Fold.
   b. Glue the x's together.
4. Glue lower jaw B to chest O. (Put glue on only one inch at the top of the underside of the jaw.)
5. Fold and glue pleat in tongue F.
6. Glue tongue F to lower jaw B. (Put glue on only one inch at the top on the underside of the tongue.)

Assemble the head.

1. Glue head A to the bag flap. (Make sure the straight edge at the base of head A is glued along the straight edge at the bottom of the bag flap.)
2. Fold nose D and glue bottom edges together. Glue nose D to head A.
3. Fold ears N and glue to head A.
4. Assemble eyes:
   a. Glue irises GG to eyewhites G.
   b. Glue pupils H to eyewhites G.
5. Glue assembled eyes to head A.
6. Fold eyebrows I. Glue back of folded eyebrows I to head A.
7. Cut all the slits on hat R.
8. Shape top of hat R by putting glue in the triangle next to the slit at the center top of the hat. Overlap the slit edge to the dotted line and press.
9. Wrap ends of cut strips of hat R around a pencil to curl.
10. Glue hat R to head A.

Macmillan/McGraw-Hill

TROLL PATTERN

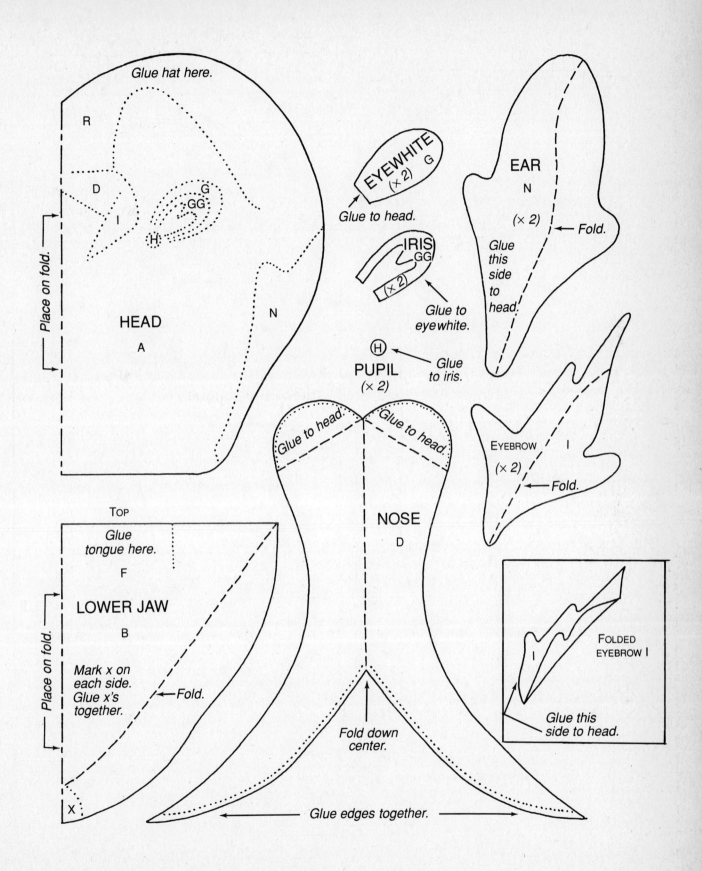

Glue hat here.

R

D

I

G
GG
H

HEAD
A

Place on fold.

N

EYEWHITE
(× 2) G

Glue to head.

IRIS
GG
(× 2)

Glue to eyewhite.

Ⓗ

PUPIL
(× 2)

Glue to iris.

EAR
N
(× 2)

Fold.

Glue this side to head.

EYEBROW
(× 2) I

Fold.

Glue to head.   Glue to head.

NOSE
D

Fold down center.

TOP

Glue tongue here.

F

LOWER JAW
B

Mark x on each side. Glue x's together.

Fold.

Place on fold.

X

Glue edges together.

FOLDED EYEBROW I

I

Glue this side to head.

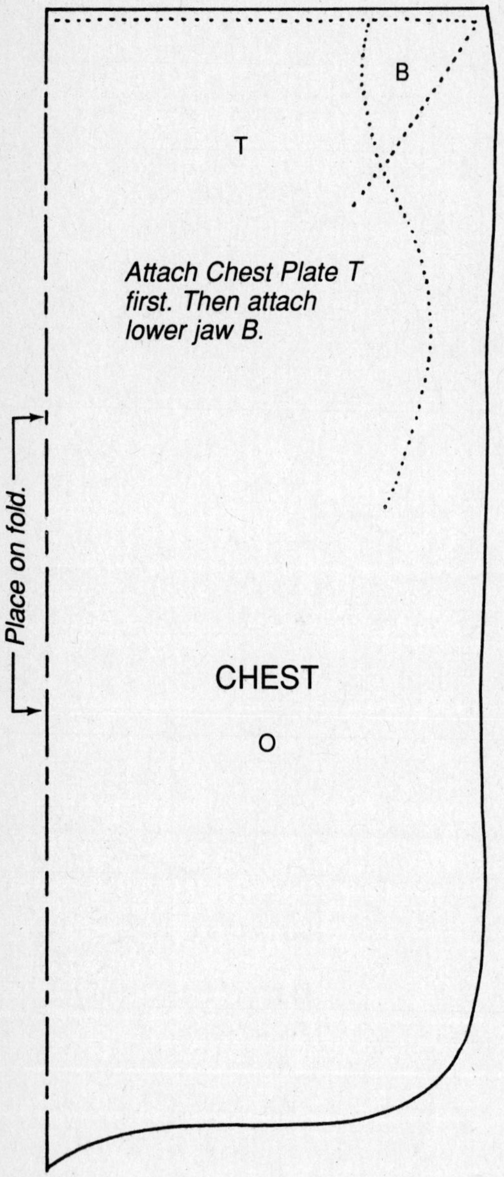

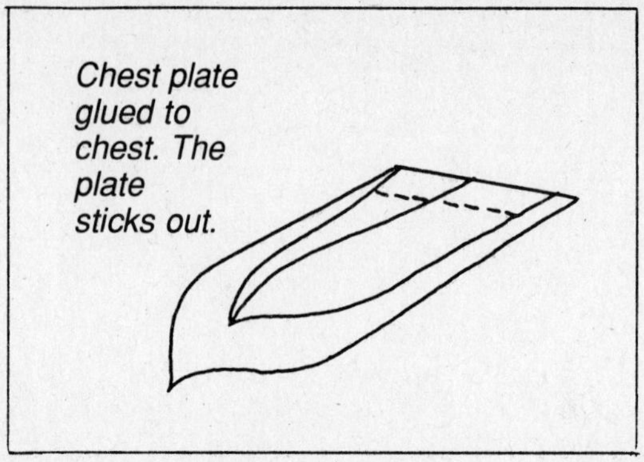

Chest plate glued to chest. The plate sticks out.

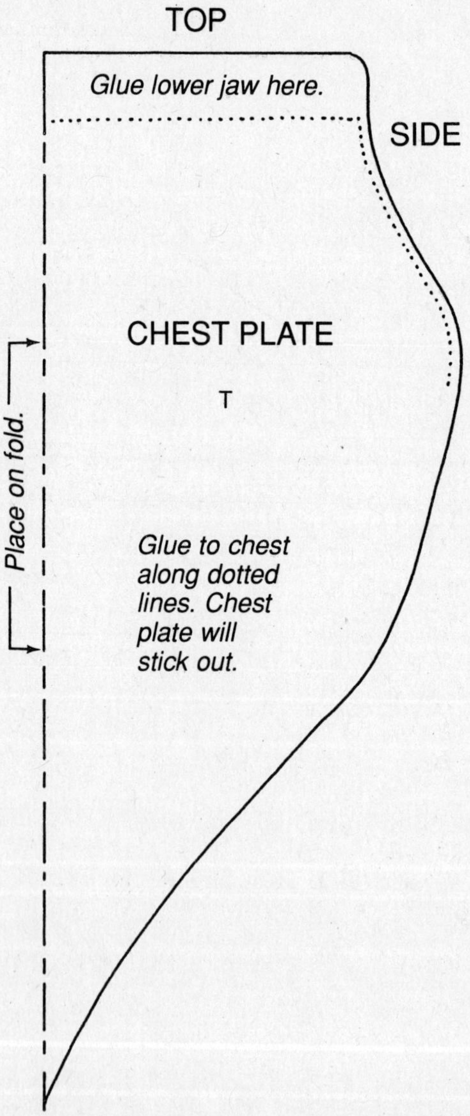

Attach Chest Plate T first. Then attach lower jaw B.

B

T

Place on fold.

CHEST

O

TOP

Glue lower jaw here.

SIDE

CHEST PLATE

T

Place on fold.

Glue to chest along dotted lines. Chest plate will stick out.

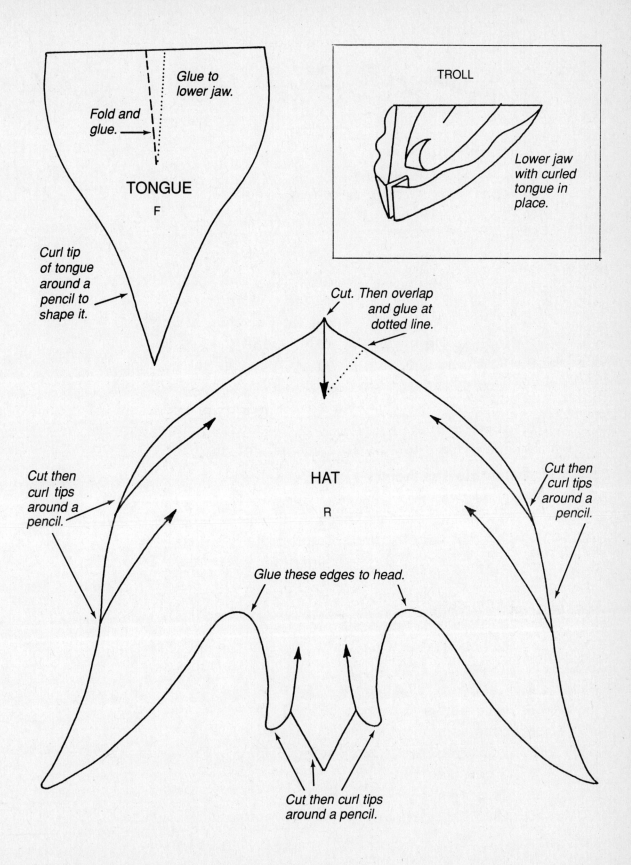

TROLL

Lower jaw with curled tongue in place.

Glue to lower jaw.

Fold and glue.

TONGUE

F

Curl tip of tongue around a pencil to shape it.

Cut. Then overlap and glue at dotted line.

HAT

R

Cut then curl tips around a pencil.

Cut then curl tips around a pencil.

Glue these edges to head.

Cut then curl tips around a pencil.

GOBLIN

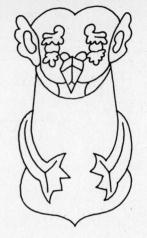

Assemble the body.

1. Glue arms V under chest O.
2. Glue chest O to body of bag.
3. Form lower jaw B:
   a. Fold.
   b. Cut each slit.
   c. Put glue in the triangle next to each slit. Overlap the slit edge to the dotted line and press.
4. Glue lower jaw B to chest O. (Put glue on only one inch at the top of the underside of the jaw.)
5. Fold tongue F. Cut slit in tip. Put glue in the triangle next to the slit. Overlap the slit edge to the dotted line and press.
6. Glue tongue F to lower jaw B. (Put glue on only one inch at the top on the underside of the tongue.)

Assemble the head.

1. Glue head A to the bag flap. (Make sure the straight edge at the base of head A is glued along the straight edge at the bottom of the bag flap.)
2. Fold nose D and glue x's together. Glue nose D to head A.
3. Form ears N:
   a. Score and cut a slit.
   b. Put glue in the triangle next to the slit. Overlap the slit edge to the dotted line and press.
4. Glue ears N to head A.
5. Glue pupils H to eyewhites G.
6. Glue assembled eyes to head A.
7. Fold eyebrows I. Wrap top of folded eyebrows around a pencil to curl.
8. Glue eyebrows I to head A.
9. Glue lower eyelashes J to eyewhites G and head A.

Macmillan/McGraw-Hill

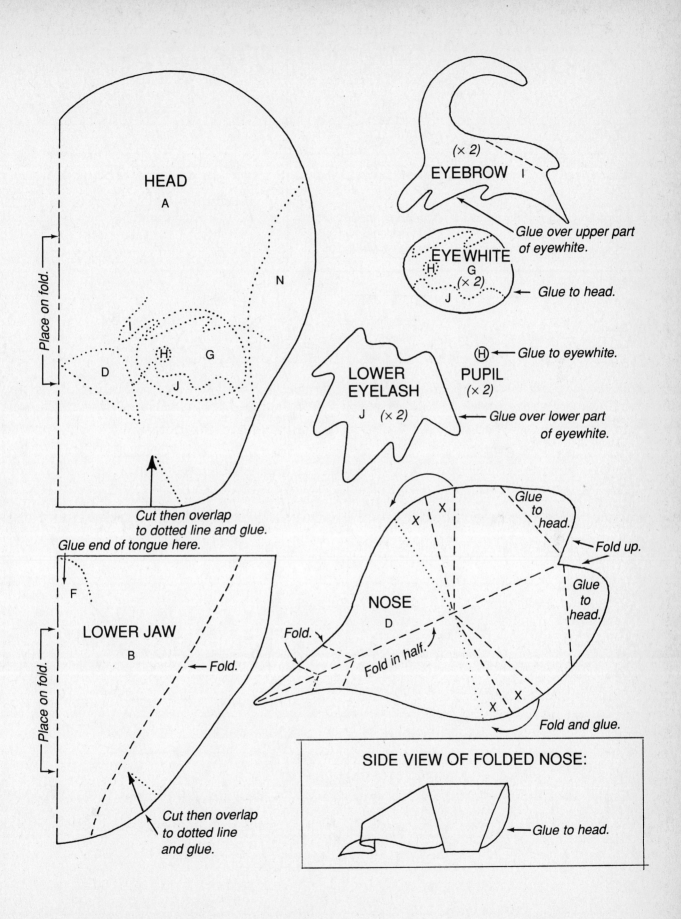

HEAD

A

N

Place on fold.

I

H   G

D

J

Cut then overlap
to dotted line and glue.
Glue end of tongue here.

EYEBROW I (× 2)

Glue over upper part
of eyewhite.

EYEWHITE
H   G
(× 2)
J

← Glue to head.

Ⓗ ← Glue to eyewhite.

**LOWER
EYELASH**

PUPIL
(× 2)

J   (× 2)

← Glue over lower part
of eyewhite.

LOWER JAW

F

B

Place on fold.

← Fold.

Cut then overlap
to dotted line
and glue.

NOSE

D

X X

Glue
to
head.

Fold up.

Glue
to
head.

Fold.

Fold in half.

X X

Fold and glue.

SIDE VIEW OF FOLDED NOSE:

← Glue to head.

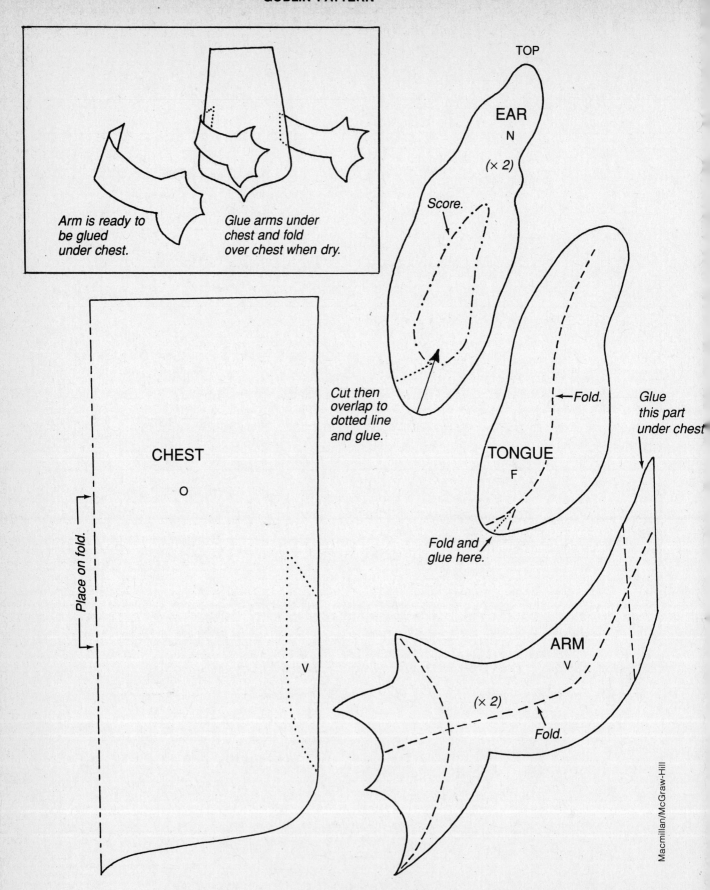

Arm is ready to be glued under chest.

Glue arms under chest and fold over chest when dry.

TOP

EAR

N

(× 2)

Score.

Cut then overlap to dotted line and glue.

CHEST

O

Place on fold.

V

Fold.

TONGUE

F

Fold and glue here.

Glue this part under chest

ARM

V

(× 2)

Fold.

Macmillan/McGraw-Hill

Dragon

Assemble the body.

1. Glue wings TT under chest O.
2. Glue chest O to body of bag.
3. Form lower jaw B:
   a. Cut slit on lower jaw B.
   b. Put glue in the triangle next to the slit. Overlap the slit edge to the dotted line and press.
4. Glue lower jaw B to chest O. (Put glue on only one inch at the top of the underside of the jaw.)
5. Wrap pointed tip of tongue F around a pencil to curl.
6. Glue tongue F to lower jaw B. (Put glue on only one inch at the top on the underside of the tongue.)
7. Glue one set of teeth FF at the front of lower jaw B. (Put glue on only 1/2 inch of the base of the teeth.)

Assemble the head.

1. Cut slits on the left and right bottom of head A. To form the nose put glue in the triangle next to each slit. Overlap the slit edge to the dotted line and press.
2. Cut a slit in the top of head A.
3. Glue head A to the bag flap. Spread apart the sides of the slit cut at the top of head A so a V-shape is formed. This will make the nose stand out from the bag.
4. Shape nostrils D by gluing the x's together.
5. Glue nostrils D to head A.
6. Glue eyebrows I to head A. Wrap the tops of the eyebrows I around a pencil to curl.
7. Shape eyewhites G by gluing the x's together.
8. Glue eyewhites G to eyebrows I.
9. Glue pupils H to eyewhites G.
10. Glue one set of teeth FF below the nostrils D on the inside of head A.
11. Glue mane M over the V shape at the top of head A. Wrap the ends of the mane M around a pencil to curl.

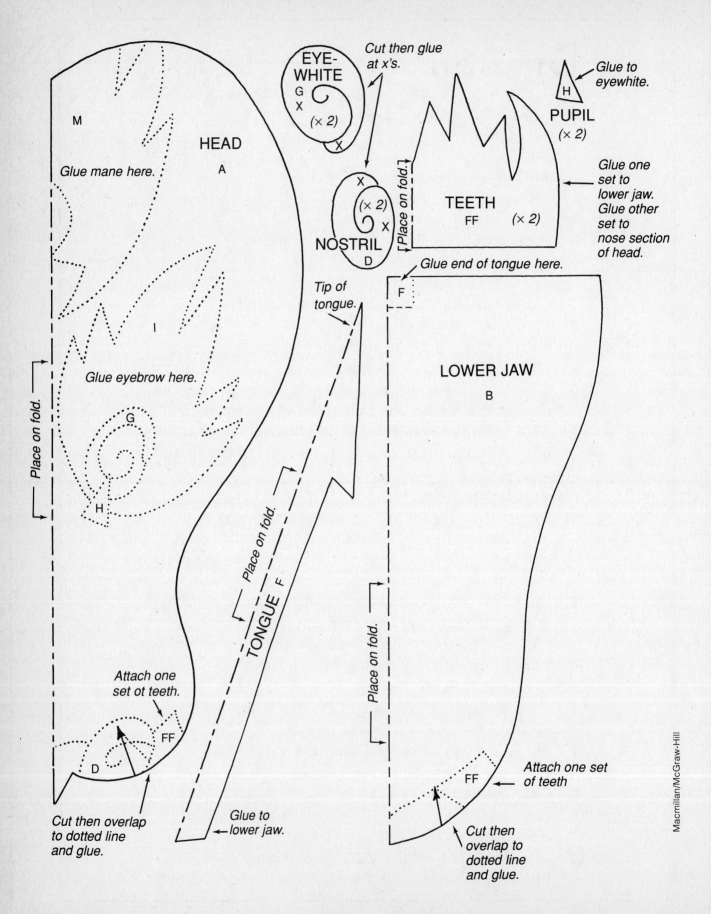

EYE-
WHITE

G
X

(× 2)

X

*Cut then glue
at x's.*

X

(× 2)

X

NOSTRIL

D

Place on fold.

TEETH

FF   (× 2)

H

*Glue to
eyewhite.*

PUPIL

(× 2)

*Glue one
set to
lower jaw.
Glue other
set to
nose section
of head.*

M

HEAD

A

Glue mane here.

I

Glue eyebrow here.

G

H

Place on fold.

*Tip of
tongue.*

F

Glue end of tongue here.

LOWER JAW

B

Place on fold.

Place on fold.

TONGUE F

*Attach one
set ot teeth.*

FF

D

*Cut then overlap
to dotted line
and glue.*

*Glue to
lower jaw.*

FF

*Attach one set
of teeth*

*Cut then
overlap to
dotted line
and glue.*

Macmillan/McGraw-Hill

DRAGON PATTERN

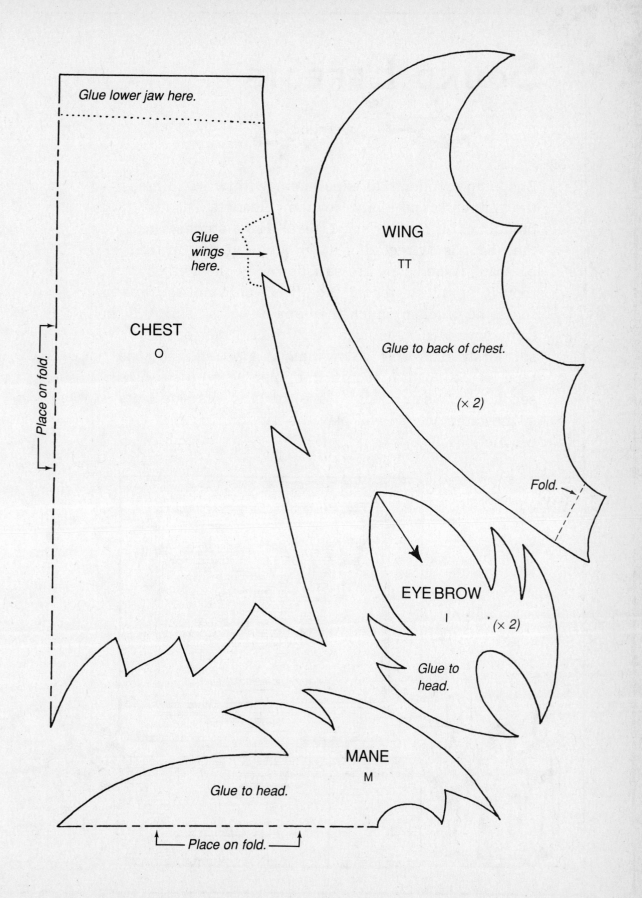

Glue lower jaw here.

Glue wings here.

CHEST

O

Place on fold.

WING

TT

Glue to back of chest.

(× 2)

Fold.

EYE BROW

I (× 2)

Glue to head.

MANE

M

Glue to head.

Place on fold.

Sound Effects

Encourage students to experiment with ways to create the various sound effects for their Readers Theater production of *Castles and Quests*. Have students test their sounds by recording them and listening to the playback. When they are satisfied with the sounds they've produced, record the effects on a master tape in the same order in which they appear in the script. If the same sound effect is used more than once, record it separately each time. Allow time to start and stop the tape by letting the recorder run silently for about five seconds between effects. Have the students select a sound director who will play the tape during the production.

Macmillan/McGraw-Hill

The Breath of Life

By Judith Bauer Stamper

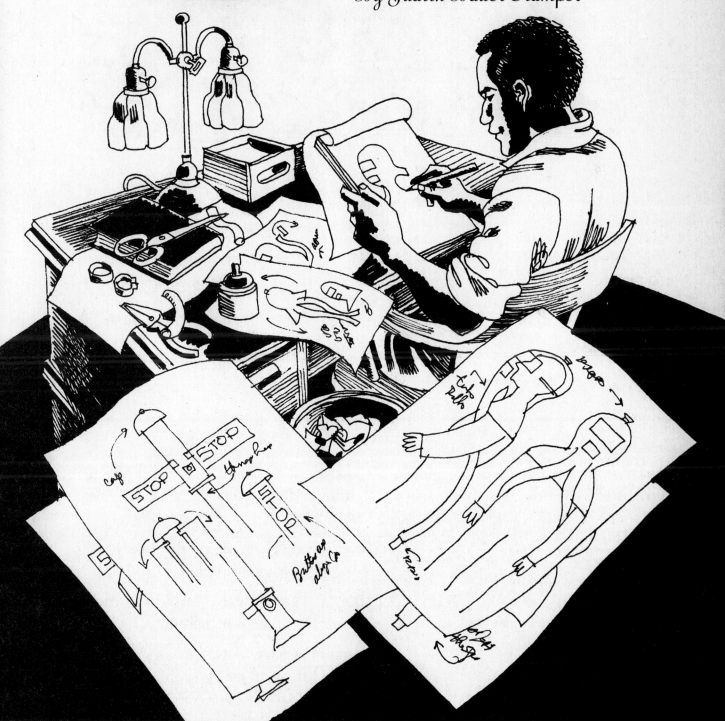

CAST

NARRATOR	ENGINEER RHINEHALT	LORA KELLY
MARY ANNE MORGAN	SANDHOG 1	FRANK MORGAN
GARRETT MORGAN	MESSENGER	SANDHOG 2
SUPERINTENDENT VAN DUZEN	TOM CLANCY	SANDHOG 3
MRS. VAN DUZEN	COMMISSIONER JAEGER	WILLIAM VAN DUZEN
PATRICK SULLIVAN	FIRE CHIEF WALLACE	CITIZEN 1
EDITOR	JOHN MURRAY	CITIZEN 2
PAUL EDWARDS		

NARRATOR: It was July 25, 1916, and the citizens of Cleveland, Ohio, were suffering from a heat wave. Garrett Morgan had gone to bed early, exhausted by the heat and a hard day at work. Setting up a new business like his National Safety Device Company wasn't easy. Suddenly, something woke Morgan and his wife, Mary Anne, from a sound sleep.

MARY ANNE MORGAN: What . . . what's the matter, Garrett?

GARRETT MORGAN: I don't know. Something woke me up—some sound. There it is again.

NARRATOR: Half asleep, the two peered out the bedroom window.

MARY ANNE MORGAN: The sky is so bright! I wonder if it's heat lightning.

GARRETT MORGAN: No, it looks more like rocket flares to me. There's another one streaking across the sky! Did you see it? That's what woke us up.

MARY ANNE MORGAN: It must be someone who doesn't know the Fourth of July is over.

GARRETT MORGAN: I don't think so, Mary Anne. I think those rockets are a distress signal.

MARY ANNE MORGAN: Can you tell where they're coming from?

GARRETT MORGAN: Hmmm. . . . They seem to be coming from the direction of Lake Erie. Could be it's from the site of that new tunnel the Water Works is digging under the lake bed. They work around the clock out there.

MARY ANNE MORGAN: Oh, dear. If there's trouble in the tunnel, that could be very bad.

NARRATOR: While Garrett and Mary Anne Morgan were wondering what had happened, one man was finding out—a man by the name of Gustav Van Duzen, construction superintendent for the Cleveland Water Works. He and his wife were awakened, too—by the ringing of the telephone.

SUPT. VAN DUZEN: Who could be calling at this hour? It's after midnight!

MRS. VAN DUZEN: I hope it's not bad news.

SUPT. VAN DUZEN: Hello . . . hello? Who is this?

PATRICK SULLIVAN: Van! Thank goodness you're home! This is Patrick Sullivan. We've had a terrible accident at Crib 5! There was a gas explosion in the tunnel, and the crew is trapped!

SUPT. VAN DUZEN: Oh, no! I'll take the next tugboat out to the crib. Make sure that *no one* goes down into that tunnel until I get there. It's probably full of poisonous gas.

PATRICK SULLIVAN: It's too late, Van. Superintendent Johnston went down as soon as he knew there was something wrong. I don't know if he's come back up yet. I had to leave the crib to come ashore to call you.

SUPT. VAN DUZEN: All right, Sullivan, take it easy now. I'm on my way.

PATRICK SULLIVAN: Yes, sir, and please hurry! It's pandemonium out there!

MRS. VAN DUZEN: What's wrong, Gustav?

SUPT. VAN DUZEN: There's been an explosion at Crib 5. I've got to get out there right away.

MRS. VAN DUZEN: Gustav, please be careful!

NARRATOR: In another part of the city, the newsroom of the *Cleveland Plain Dealer* was buzzing with reports of the tragedy.

EDITOR: Edwards, come into my office! I just talked to the police chief. Your hunch about those rockets was right.

PAUL EDWARDS: So they *were* from the Water Works project.

EDITOR: Yes! A gas explosion ripped through the new tunnel they're digging. It's a disaster. There isn't a minute to lose. I want you to go out to Crib 5 right away. Get the story and call it in to me for the morning edition.

PAUL EDWARDS: Right, boss. I'll leave immediately for the crib.

EDITOR: Oh, Edwards, one more thing—the police chief said the tug *Lorain* would be leaving from the pier in ten minutes. He thought Superintendent Van Duzen might be on board. If he is, be sure to get an interview with him.

PAUL EDWARDS: You can count on me, boss. I'm on my way!

EDITOR: Good! Now hurry; that tug will be leaving any minute.

NARRATOR: The *Lorain* was waiting to take its passengers out to Crib 5, the site of the disaster. The night air crackled with tension as Superintendent Van Duzen, a crew of rescue workers, and the news reporter scrambled on board. With a blast of its horn, the tug pulled out onto the dark waters of Lake Erie.

PAUL EDWARDS: Excuse me, sir, are you Superintendent Van Duzen?

SUPT. VAN DUZEN: Yes, I am. But I don't recognize you; are you with the rescue crew?

PAUL EDWARDS: No, I'm Paul Edwards, a reporter for the *Cleveland Plain Dealer*. I'm covering the tunnel disaster for my newspaper. Is it true that there have been casualties, and if so, how many?

SUPT. VAN DUZEN: I'm afraid the answer to your first question is yes. As for how many, . . . we don't know yet.

PAUL EDWARDS: Can you tell me what caused the explosion, sir? What went wrong?

SUPT. VAN DUZEN: I'm not sure. I just heard the news a few minutes ago myself. It looks bad, though.

PAUL EDWARDS: Maybe you could fill me in on some background information. I know our readers will be interested.

SUPT. VAN DUZEN: Well, Mr. Edwards, it's a little hard to concentrate, I'm sure you understand, but I'll try.

PAUL EDWARDS: Thank you, sir. First, would you please explain how the tunnel is being constructed?

SUPT. VAN DUZEN: Crib 5 is about four miles offshore. The crib itself is actually a big wooden structure built atop rocks that were hauled to the site and dumped into Lake Erie. It's like a little community, with a mess hall and a recreation room. There are even sleeping bunks for when the weather's bad and the crew can't get home. But the crib's main purpose is to serve as headquarters for the work on the tunnel.

PAUL EDWARDS: So the tunnel is dug from the crib, Superintendent?

SUPT. VAN DUZEN: No, not exactly. You see, there's a shaft from the crib that leads down to the tunnel. It goes—here, give me your notebook, and I'll sketch it for you.

PAUL EDWARDS: Thank you, that would be a big help.

[*Display transparency showing cross-section of Crib 5 and tunnel, page 75.*]

SUPT. VAN DUZEN: Here's Crib 5—right on the surface of the lake, see? Under it is a shaft that goes down 128 feet, right into the mud, sand, and clay under the lake.

PAUL EDWARDS: How do the men get down to the tunnel?

SUPT. VAN DUZEN: There's a lift—it looks like a cage—that takes the sandhogs down and brings them back up.

PAUL EDWARDS: "Sandhogs"?

SUPT. VAN DUZEN: That's what we call workers who tunnel under water. To get to the digging area itself, they have to go through two air locks. The tunnel is just on the other side of those air locks.

PAUL EDWARDS: Is that where the men were when the explosion took place—in the digging area?

SUPT. VAN DUZEN: Yes. When they were digging, they must have hit a large pocket of natural gas that exploded.

[*Transparency off.*]

PAUL EDWARDS: Being a sandhog sounds like dangerous work to me!

SUPT. VAN DUZEN: It is. Those men risk their lives every time they go down into that tunnel. Keeping the people of Cleveland supplied with water is a risky business.

PAUL EDWARDS: Isn't there any safety equipment for emergencies of this kind?

SUPT. VAN DUZEN: Not really. There are pulmotors, of course, but it's not customary to keep them on a crib. Perhaps that will change now.

PAUL EDWARDS: What's a pulmotor?

SUPT. VAN DUZEN: It's a device that forces oxygen into the lungs when a person has been overcome by smoke or gas. What we really need is for someone to invent a contraption that would allow us to breathe when there's gas in the tunnels. Then we could save lives when accidents such as this happen. You'll have to excuse me now, Mr. Edwards. We're about to dock, and I have my men to see to.

NARRATOR: The tug pulled up to Crib 5 at 1:30 in the morning. As the waves splashed up around the platform, Superintendent Van Duzen, known to many of his men as Old Van, leaped from the tug. Engineer Rhinehalt rushed up to him.

ENGINEER: Old Van! Thank goodness you're here!

SUPT. VAN DUZEN: I see Superintendent Johnston and Peter McKenna are over there on stretchers. You'd better tell me what happened.

ENGINEER: To make a long story short, as soon as we realized something was wrong in the tunnel, Johnston went down the shaft to investigate. Six of the men insisted on going with him. A few minutes later, we heard them tapping a distress signal on the pipe, so we knew they were in trouble.

SUPT. VAN DUZEN: The area was probably filled with gas.

ENGINEER: We were sure it was, but two more men volunteered to go down to help the others out. They found McKenna trying to drag Johnston back to the cage. Johnston was unconscious, and McKenna was almost out himself. Somehow, the four of them managed to get into the cage and come back up, but Johnston is still unconscious.

SUPT. VAN DUZEN: Are you using a pulmotor to revive him?

ENGINEER: We sent for some, but they haven't arrived yet.

SUPT. VAN DUZEN: Get a launch to take Johnston and McKenna to the hospital right away! Now, what about the rest of the men who went down with them?

ENGINEER: We don't know. There hasn't been any more tapping. It looks bad. A lot of the other men wanted to go in after them, but you said no one else should go down the shaft.

SUPT. VAN DUZEN: They'll get their chance now. I'm going down to see about those other five men!

ENGINEER: But Van, you don't have any safety equipment. That tunnel is filled with gas. You don't stand a chance!

SUPT. VAN DUZEN: The sandhogs down there don't have any safety equipment, either. Some of them may still be alive. I've *got* to go!

PATRICK SULLIVAN: I'll go with you, Van. I'd want somebody to come after me if I was trapped down there.

SANDHOG 1: I'm coming, too. My brother's in that tunnel!

SUPT. VAN DUZEN: All right then, let's get in the cage, men. Rhinehalt, send us down.

NARRATOR: The men on the crib watched in tense silence as Van Duzen and twelve other men disappeared from sight.

PAUL EDWARDS: Those are brave men. They don't know what they'll find down there.

ENGINEER: Or if they'll ever see the light of day again. We'd better be quiet and listen now. They'll tap on the pipe when they're ready for me to raise the cage.

NARRATOR: Minute after agonizing minute crept by. The minutes turned into hours, but still there was no signal from the rescue party. It was impossible to know how far into the tunnel they had gone. A feeling of overwhelming gloom settled over Crib 5.

ENGINEER: They should have been out long ago. That makes a total of twenty-nine men we've lost down there.

NARRATOR: Word of the latest calamity on Crib 5 spread quickly. A messenger was sent to notify Mrs. Van Duzen of the tragic developments.

MESSENGER: Mrs. Van Duzen? I'm sorry to bring you bad news, ma'am. Your husband led a rescue party down into the tunnel a few hours ago. They . . . they haven't been heard from since.

MRS. VAN DUZEN: Oh, no! I must call my son right away.

NARRATOR: To the frantic woman, it seemed as if the phone rang forever before a sleepy Tom Clancy answered.

TOM CLANCY: Hello?

MRS. VAN DUZEN: Tom, listen to me! Your stepfather is trapped in the tunnel of Crib 5. Hire a boat right away. Pay whatever you have to, but get out there as fast as you can. And be careful, Son!

TOM CLANCY: I'm leaving right now, Mother. I'll call you as soon as I know anything.

NARRATOR: At the same time, the news about Van Duzen and his rescue party reached the main office of the Water Works. It was quickly relayed to a group of city officials who were meeting to discuss the disaster. Water Works Commissioner Jaeger outlined the problem to his assistant John Murray and to Fire Chief Wallace.

COMMISSIONER: This is the worst tunnel accident we've ever had! Let's face it, we just aren't prepared to deal with poison gas. It's got our rescue operations beat. If only there were some kind of safety apparatus designed to prevent suffocation. Your fire-fighters need this kind of safety equipment as much as we do, Chief Wallace. Isn't there something that could help?

FIRE CHIEF: Wait a minute. What you said reminds me of something I saw in New Orleans a couple of years ago. There was a demonstration of a helmet—I believe it was called a breathing helmet . . . or maybe a safety hood. Anyway, the device was only in the testing stages, but the demonstration was pretty impressive.

COMMISSIONER: What was the demonstration?

FIRE CHIEF: They set up a canvas tent out in a field. Then they started a fire inside it. The fuel they used gave off the thickest, most poisonous smoke imaginable. The tent was very well secured so that fresh air couldn't get in, and the smoke couldn't get out.

COMMISSIONER: And I suppose you're going to tell me that someone actually went inside that tent and lived to tell about it.

FIRE CHIEF: Commissioner Jaeger, that's exactly what happened! They sent in a man fitted with one of these safety hoods. The smoke was so thick you could practically cut it, but that man stayed inside the tent for a full twenty minutes. When he came out, he was fine. He even gave another demonstration a little later on.

COMMISSIONER: That's incredible! I wonder if they ever tested the hood with poison gas.

FIRE CHIEF: As I recall, they read a letter from the president of a refrigeration plant. The plant uses ammonia gas in their process, which, of course, is highly toxic. According to the letter, the same man tested the safety hood in a room filled with ammonia gas. So did the president of the company. Both came out of the room perfectly fit!

JOHN MURRAY: Now that you mention it, Chief Wallace, I remember reading about the inventor of that hood a couple of years ago. He won first prize and a gold medal at an international safety exposition in New York City. He's a black man by the name of Morris . . . no . . . Moran? . . . Morgan? That's it, Morgan! And as I recall, he lives right here in Cleveland!

COMMISSIONER: Murray, I want you to find out his full name and get hold of him—on the double! Ask him to round up as many of those safety hoods of his as possible. Tell him we need them out on Crib 5.

FIRE CHIEF: And if Morgan is willing to come out to the crib himself, tell him that we'll meet him there. I'll make sure a tug is waiting to take him.

JOHN MURRAY: Good idea! He sounds like the kind of man we need at the scene. This may be our only chance to save the rescue party.

NARRATOR: Just before dawn, there was a knock at Garrett Morgan's door.

JOHN MURRAY: Mr. Morgan? I'm John Murray from the Water Works. I'm Commissioner Jaeger's assistant. I've come to ask for your help.

GARRETT MORGAN: Would this have anything to do with those rocket flares I saw around midnight?

JOHN MURRAY: Unfortunately, yes. There was an explosion in the tunnel being dug under the lake. A rescue crew is trapped down there. Fire Chief Wallace thinks that if we had some of your hoods, we could go into the tunnel and get the men out. Otherwise, they don't stand a chance.

GARRETT MORGAN: I'll bring all the hoods I have. Let's stop on the way and pick up my brother Frank—he's familiar with the way my safety hood operates.

MARY ANNE MORGAN: Garrett, please be careful!

GARRETT MORGAN: Don't worry, Mary Anne. Come on, Mr. Murray, we don't have a minute to spare!

NARRATOR: The sun was just rising over Lake Erie as Murray, accompanied by Garrett and Frank Morgan, arrived at the pier. The three of them boarded the tug along with doctors, other rescue workers, and William Van Duzen, Superintendent Van Duzen's younger son. Reporter Lora Kelly was also on board.

LORA KELLY: Mr. Morgan, I'm Lora Kelly from the *Cleveland Plain Dealer*. I understand you've brought along one of your inventions. How can it help save the men trapped in the tunnel?

GARRETT MORGAN: The device is called a safety hood. It allows rescue workers to breathe fresh air in areas filled with smoke and gas. We'll use the hoods to go into the tunnel where the rescue party is trapped. I just hope we're in time.

LORA KELLY: You said *we*, Mr. Morgan. Do you mean that you're planning to go down into that tunnel yourself?

GARRETT MORGAN: Yes, of course—my brother and I will both go. The other rescue parties had no breathing apparatus. They didn't stand a chance in that poisonous air. But Frank and I will be all right.

Macmillan/McGraw-Hill

LORA KELLY: Just how does your safety hood work, Mr. Morgan? It sounds as though you're staking your life on it.

GARRETT MORGAN: I think the easiest way to explain it, Miss Kelly, is by showing you one.

LORA KELLY: That would be wonderful, Mr. Morgan. If you don't mind, I'll sketch it for my newspaper.

[*Display transparency of Morgan's Safety Hood, page 76.*]

GARRETT MORGAN: As you can see, the hood totally covers the head and protects it from gas and smoke. The person wearing it breathes normally through these two tubes. A supply of filtered air comes in through this tube, and exhaled air goes out through a valve in the other tube.

LORA KELLY: What's this at the end of the tube, Mr. Morgan? It looks like a sponge.

GARRETT MORGAN: That's just what it is, ma'am. When we wet the sponge, it prevents smoke and dust from going up into the tube. It also cools the air.

[*Transparency off.*]

LORA KELLY: Mr. Morgan, I have a feeling that after today, your name will be known to everyone in Cleveland. Our readers will surely want to know a lot more about you. Were you born here in Cleveland?

GARRETT MORGAN: No, I come from Paris, Kentucky. I was one of eleven children.

LORA KELLY: Did your whole family move to Ohio?

GARRETT MORGAN: No, I left home when I was fourteen. I'd finished elementary school, but there didn't seem to be much opportunity for me in Paris, Kentucky. So I came to Cleveland. Let me tell you, I'll never forget the day I arrived. One thin dime was all the money I had in the world!

LORA KELLY: What did you do?

GARRETT MORGAN: Well, ma'am, I was always mechanically inclined, so I taught myself enough about sewing machines to get a job fixing them. A few years later, I had enough money to open my own repair shop, to send for my brother, and to get married.

LORA KELLY: How do you find time to do your inventing, Mr. Morgan?

GARRETT MORGAN: I always make time for that. I invented the safety hood four years ago, in 1912. After I got a patent for it, I set up the National Safety Device Company to manufacture the hoods and sell them. We've had some success, but not as much as I had hoped for.

LORA KELLY: Well, today may change all that!

GARRETT MORGAN: Saving the lives of the men trapped in the tunnel—that's the most important thing today.

FRANK MORGAN: There's the crib up ahead, Garrett. We'd better get these hoods ready.

LORA KELLY: Good luck, to both of you.

NARRATOR: As the tugboat prepared to dock, Garrett and Frank Morgan could hear the frantic cries of those on the platform.

SANDHOG 2: Are there any doctors aboard?

SANDHOG 3: Did you bring any pulmotors?

NARRATOR: The Morgan brothers were immediately surrounded by a swarm of anxious people, including Water Works Commissioner Jaeger and Fire Chief Wallace, who had arrived by tug a short time before.

COMMISSIONER: Thank goodness you've come. From what we've been told, it's been a terrible night out here. Van Duzen's rescue party went down about five hours ago. There haven't been any signals from them since then, so we don't know if they're dead or alive.

WILLIAM: Oh, no. Dad can't be dead!

ENGINEER: I'm sorry, William. Your stepbrother, Tom, went down to look for your father. He put a wet towel over his face to block out some of the gas, but it didn't help much. It didn't stop him, though. He kept going down into that tunnel again and again.

SANDHOG 3: He rescued three men, but he couldn't get to Old Van.

SANDHOG 2: Tom said he could see through the glass porthole in the air lock. Men were lying on the ground, gasping for air. He broke the porthole glass to give them what little air there was, but that was all he could do.

ENGINEER: When he came back up, he was barely alive himself. He's doing all right now, though. He's a real hero.

WILLIAM: You're our only hope now, Mr. Morgan—you and your safety hoods.

GARRETT MORGAN: I'll do everything I can to help, son. Before I go down, though, I think it would be a good idea to talk to your stepbrother. Since he's been down to the tunnel, he can give us a better idea of what conditions are like.

NARRATOR: William took Garrett Morgan over to where Tom Clancy sat recovering from his ordeal.

WILLIAM: Tom, I'm so glad you're all right. This is Mr. Morgan—he's invented a breathing device for use with poisonous gas. He's going to wear it down in the tunnel to try to find Dad and the other men and bring them out.

GARRETT MORGAN: You're a brave man, Mr. Clancy. It took real courage to go down into that tunnel.

TOM CLANCY: I just had to, Mr. Morgan. My stepfather is down in there, but there was no way I could reach him. I couldn't get past the air lock. Looking through that porthole into the tunnel was an awful sight. I could see the men in there, but I wasn't able to help them!

GARRETT MORGAN: Can you describe what it was like in the tunnel?

TOM CLANCY: It was like being in a black hole. When I got to the air lock . . . that's when the gas really hit me. Suddenly, I could hardly breathe. I remember getting dizzy and falling down—I thought I was a goner. But there must have been a layer of air along the ground because I finally managed to crawl back to the cage.

GARRETT MORGAN: You're lucky to be alive!

NARRATOR: At that moment, a great shout came from the group of anxious watchers at the top of the shaft. It was now about 7:15 in the morning.

ENGINEER: I hear tapping! It's faint, but I can just make it out!

SANDHOG 3: They're alive! They're alive!

GARRETT MORGAN: Quick, Frank, let's put on our safety hoods. I guess this is as true a test of my invention as I'll ever have.

FRANK MORGAN: I'm trusting that the hoods will work, Garrett.

GARRETT MORGAN: If I didn't have absolute faith in this equipment, Frank, I'd never allow you to go down into that tunnel with me.

FRANK MORGAN: All right, Garrett, I'm ready.

ENGINEER: Let them through! Move aside! There's not a moment to lose!

NARRATOR: Garrett and Frank Morgan made their way through the crowd and entered the cage. With a shout of warning to the watchers, Engineer Rhinehalt lowered the cage until it came to rest at the bottom of the shaft. At that moment, William Van Duzen grabbed a hammer.

WILLIAM: We've got to let those trapped men know we heard them, so they don't lose hope.

NARRATOR: As he began to pound on the pipe, each blow of the hammer seemed to say, "Help is coming. We heard you. Have courage!" Then the nervous waiting began, as each person imagined what was taking place below.

FIRE CHIEF: Even with those safety hoods, Garrett and Frank Morgan are taking a terrible risk going into that tunnel. I pray that there isn't a second explosion.

LORA KELLY: Mr. Morgan told me they could stay down for about twenty minutes at a time. It's almost that long now. Do you think they're all right?

PAUL EDWARDS: Can you see anything of what's happening below, engineer?

ENGINEER: No, it's too dark. Wait! I hear their signal. I'm bringing up the lift. Gangway!

NARRATOR: The winding rope coiled swiftly, bringing the cage back up. It stopped with a thump, and two men staggered off. They were caked with clay from head to foot, and their wet, matted hair clung to their faces. Too dazed to move, they simply stood and stared. In the crowd, some men were crying. Others clapped and cheered.

COMMISSIONER: Someone lend a hand here! Carry these men over to the stretchers where the doctors can treat them.

ENGINEER: Hurry! I've got to send the cage back down!

NARRATOR: Down went the cage and another anxious wait began. A few minutes later, two more men were brought up to the surface and safety.

WILLIAM: Dad! It's Dad—and he's alive!

SUPT. VAN DUZEN: [*coughing*] I never thought I'd see daylight again.

NARRATOR: Garrett and Frank Morgan made many trips up and down in the lift that day. With each trip, they brought out more men. Unfortunately, not all were alive.

JOHN MURRAY: Is there any hope of reaching the crew that was actually digging the tunnel, Mr. Morgan?

GARRETT MORGAN: I'm afraid not. The walls and the ceiling of the tunnel collapsed during the explosion. It'll take days, maybe weeks, to dig through the rubble.

COMMISSIONER: Well, thank goodness you were able to bring out all the others. Those that survived owe you their lives.

PAUL EDWARDS: Excuse me, Mr. Morgan. Can we get a picture of you and your brother for our paper?

LORA KELLY: I said you'd be famous after today, and I believe I was right.

NARRATOR: For days, the newspaper carried stories about the tunnel explosion and the heroism of Garrett Morgan and the other rescue workers. The inventor became a well-known figure in the city of Cleveland.

FRANK MORGAN: Have you seen today's paper, Garrett?

GARRETT MORGAN: I'm looking at the *Plain Dealer* right now. Those two reporters really did get a picture of us. Here it is, right on the front page. Just listen to the headline: "Heroes Risk Lives to Recover Workers' Bodies."

FRANK MORGAN: There's been a big investigation of the accident. People are saying that your safety hoods should be kept at the cribs in case there are other accidents like this one.

NARRATOR: Their conversation was interrupted by a knock at the door. A messenger, carrying a large white envelope, stood on the porch.

MESSENGER: Mr. Morgan? I've been asked to deliver this to you.

GARRETT MORGAN: Why, thank you.

MARY ANNE MORGAN: What is it, Garrett?

GARRETT MORGAN: It's an invitation. Listen to this: "The grateful citizens of Cleveland invite you to attend a special ceremony in recognition of your heroism during the Water Works tunnel explosion." Well, how about that! Frank's invited, too. They want to honor both of us.

MARY ANNE MORGAN: That's wonderful! Your safety hood is finally getting the recognition it deserves.

GARRETT MORGAN: Yes. Orders for the safety hood are pouring in from all over the country. It's too bad it took such a tragedy to make people aware of it.

NARRATOR: A few days later, the three members of the Morgan family proudly set out for the ceremony in Garrett's automobile. At that time, cars were such a rarity in Cleveland that few if any traffic safety rules existed. As a result, the driving conditions were so hazardous that motorists found that it took luck as well as skill to arrive safely at their destination.

MARY ANNE MORGAN: Look up ahead. There seems to be some kind of trouble at the intersection.

FRANK MORGAN: It looks like another accident between an automobile and a horse-and-buggy. It seems that each driver always thinks the other one should stop, but lots of times neither one does.

GARRETT MORGAN: I'm afraid that it's just going to get worse as more and more people own automobiles. There must be *something* that can be done.

MARY ANNE MORGAN: Well, thank goodness we've arrived in one piece.

NARRATOR: As they made their way into the room in which the ceremony was to be held, Garrett Morgan tucked away the traffic problem into the back of his mind.

CITIZEN 1: Ladies and gentlemen, we are here today to honor Mr. Garrett Morgan not only for his heroism, but also for his invention of the safety hood. We foresee this device will mean the breath of life to every sandhog, miner, fire-fighter, and police officer across the land.

CITIZEN 2: Mr. Morgan, we take great pleasure in presenting you with this medal as a token of our gratitude and esteem. We have had it inscribed. It reads: "To Garrett A. Morgan, our most honored and bravest citizen."

GARRETT MORGAN: Thank you, I am deeply honored. I only wish that all of the men who descended into that tunnel could be here with us today. They are the ones who deserve medals.

NARRATOR: A few weeks later, Garrett and Frank were interrupted at work by a commotion on the street. They rushed out to see what had happened.

FRANK MORGAN: There's been another accident between an automobile and a horse-and-buggy. These intersections are getting more and more dangerous. Something has to be done!

GARRETT MORGAN: Hmmm. . . . There must be a way to keep traffic in order. Maybe a signal—a special kind of mechanical traffic-signaling device that would indicate whose turn it was to proceed. . . . Perhaps it could even use lights. That just might be the answer. . . .

NARRATOR: In the years that followed, Garrett Morgan's safety hood received wider and wider recognition. During World War I, Morgan improved the hood, and it became a mask that could be used in combat. The gas mask, as it was then called, became standard equipment for every soldier in the field; it is credited with saving hundreds of thousands of lives on the battlefields of Europe. At the same time, Garrett Morgan's inventive mind was busily working on other problems. In 1923, he obtained a patent on what would become his most widely used invention—the traffic light. In later years, Morgan became active in local politics. He also started his own newspaper for the black community in Cleveland. When he died in 1963 at the age of eighty-six, Garrett Morgan left a proud legacy behind him. Thanks to his efforts, the world is a better and safer place in which to live.

BLOCKING
DIAGRAM

Arrange twenty-one chairs, as shown. The narrator can use a music stand to hold the script.

1. NARRATOR
2. MESSENGER
3. PAUL EDWARDS
4. LORA KELLY
5. FRANK MORGAN
6. GARRETT MORGAN
7. SUPT. VAN DUZEN
8. ENGINEER RHINEHALT
9. JOHN MURRAY
10. COMMISSIONER JAEGER
11. FIRE CHIEF WALLACE

12. EDITOR
13. CITIZEN 1
14. CITIZEN 2
15. MARY ANNE MORGAN
16. MRS. VAN DUZEN
17. WILLIAM VAN DUZEN
18. TOM CLANCY
19. PAT SULLIVAN
20. SANDHOG 1
21. SANDHOG 2
22. SANDHOG 3

Reproduce the patterns, pages 75 and 76, onto acetate to create overhead transparencies. Following the cues in the script, project them onto a light-colored wall or screen behind the cast.

CLEVELAND
WATER WORKS TUNNEL

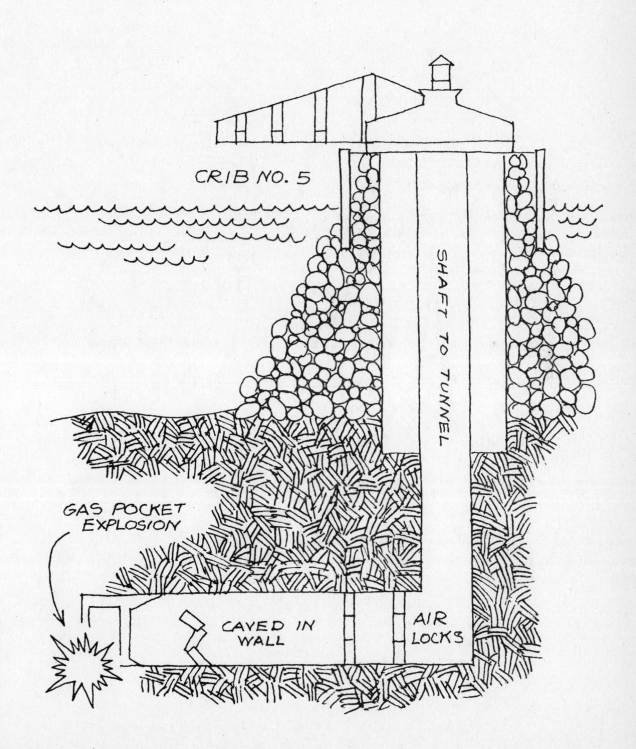

CRIB NO. 5

SHAFT TO TUNNEL

GAS POCKET
EXPLOSION

CAVED IN
WALL

AIR
LOCKS

GARRETT MORGAN'S
SAFETY HOOD

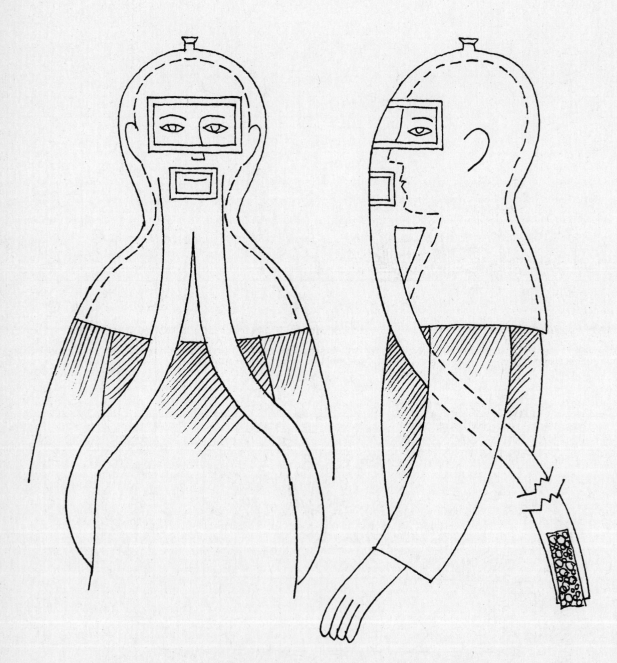

Macmillan/McGraw-Hill

THE CASE OF THE UNCOOKED EGGS

BY MYKA-LYNN SOKOLOFF, BASED ON A HAITIAN FOLK TALE

CAST

BUS DRIVER	FARMER
NICOLE	MESSENGER
MONIQUE	SCHOOLTEACHER
ODETTE	JUDGE
JEANNE	LAWYER 1
SOLDIER	LAWYER 2
MARKET WOMAN	POOR MAN

SETTING

A SMALL TOWN IN HAITI

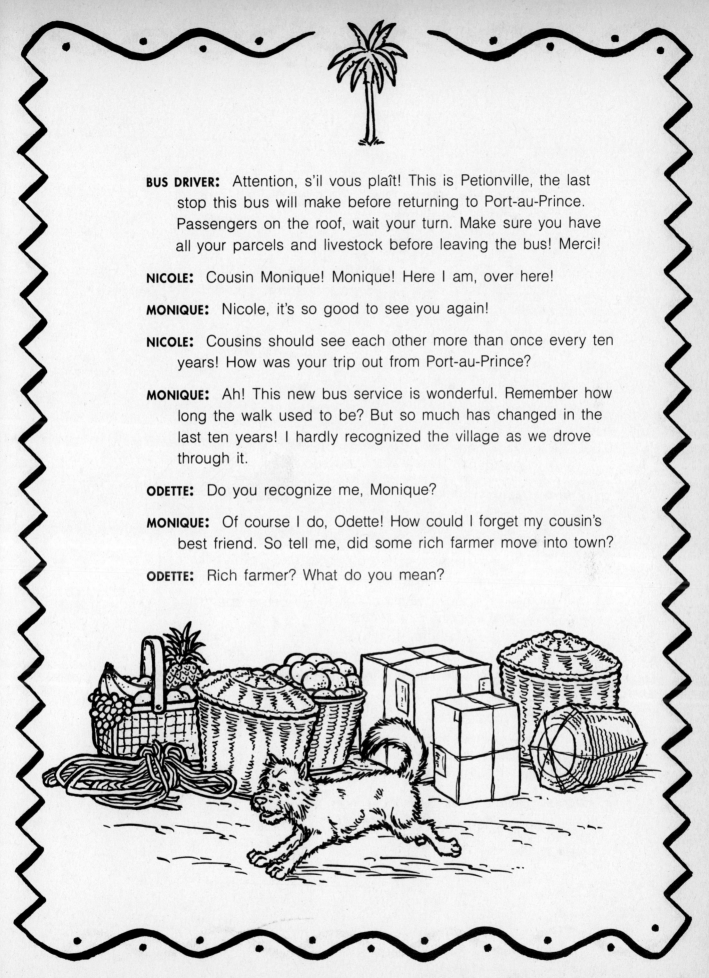

BUS DRIVER: Attention, s'il vous plaît! This is Petionville, the last stop this bus will make before returning to Port-au-Prince. Passengers on the roof, wait your turn. Make sure you have all your parcels and livestock before leaving the bus! Merci!

NICOLE: Cousin Monique! Monique! Here I am, over here!

MONIQUE: Nicole, it's so good to see you again!

NICOLE: Cousins should see each other more than once every ten years! How was your trip out from Port-au-Prince?

MONIQUE: Ah! This new bus service is wonderful. Remember how long the walk used to be? But so much has changed in the last ten years! I hardly recognized the village as we drove through it.

ODETTE: Do you recognize me, Monique?

MONIQUE: Of course I do, Odette! How could I forget my cousin's best friend. So tell me, did some rich farmer move into town?

ODETTE: Rich farmer? What do you mean?

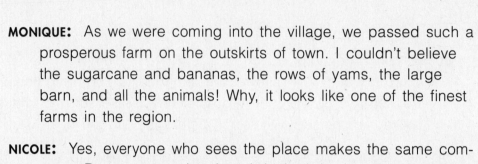

MONIQUE: As we were coming into the village, we passed such a prosperous farm on the outskirts of town. I couldn't believe the sugarcane and bananas, the rows of yams, the large barn, and all the animals! Why, it looks like one of the finest farms in the region.

NICOLE: Yes, everyone who sees the place makes the same comment. Do you remember how it looked the last time you were here?

MONIQUE: I certainly do! What a ramshackle place it was—just a small, thatched shack with a leaky roof and a crumbling, old barn. As I remember, it belonged to a poor widow whose name was Jeanne. How did this transformation take place?

NICOLE: Ah, that's one of my favorite stories! Odette and I will tell it to you as we walk home. You see, it all started like this. . . .

SOUND EFFECT: [*knocking on door*]

JEANNE: Bonjour, soldier. How can I help you?

SOLDIER: Bonjour, madame. I'm on leave and on my way home to visit my family. I've been walking all day, but I still have many kilometers to go. I was wondering if I could spend the night in your barn?

JEANNE: Oui, but of course! It's an old barn that leaks when it rains; however, some shelter is better than none at all. But first, come in and have a bite of supper with me. It's only a simple meal—beans and rice—but I would be pleased to have you share it with me.

SOLDIER: Merci. That's very kind of you.

NICOLE: Before leaving the next morning, the soldier stopped at Jeanne's house to thank her for her hospitality.

SOLDIER: I have no money to pay you for your kindness, but I hope you'll accept these three eggs I happen to have in my knapsack. Perhaps you'll cook them for your breakfast. Au revoir, madame, and thank you again.

NICOLE: And with that, the soldier tipped his cap and went on his way.

JEANNE: Three eggs! Ah, they'd make a fine omelette, and, to tell the truth, I am a bit hungry. But, on the other hand, if I put them under a hen for a few days, perhaps they'll hatch. Yes, that's what I'll do.

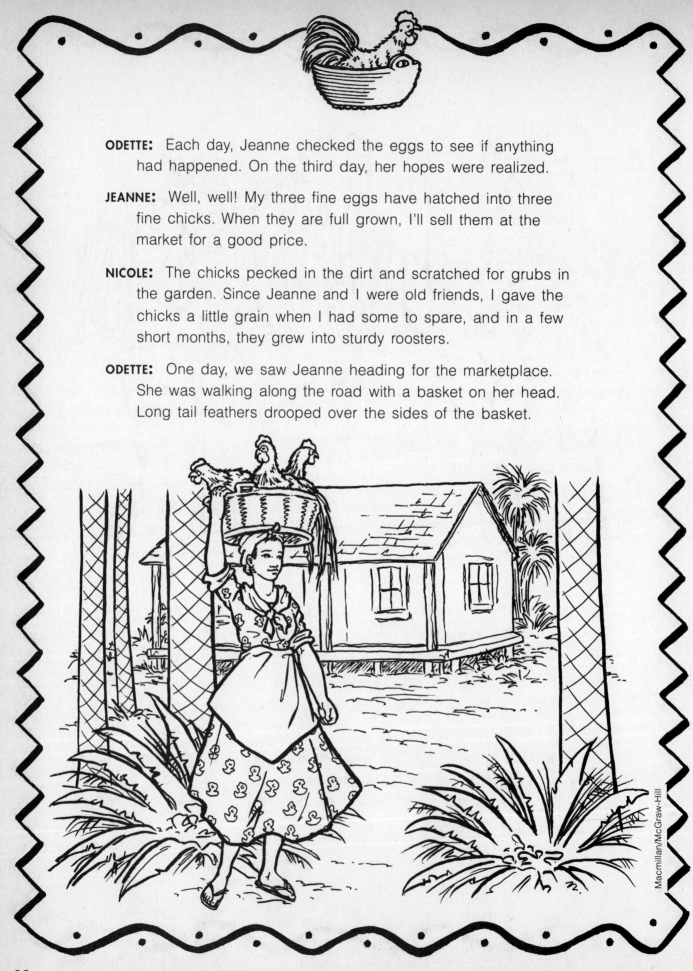

ODETTE: Each day, Jeanne checked the eggs to see if anything had happened. On the third day, her hopes were realized.

JEANNE: Well, well! My three fine eggs have hatched into three fine chicks. When they are full grown, I'll sell them at the market for a good price.

NICOLE: The chicks pecked in the dirt and scratched for grubs in the garden. Since Jeanne and I were old friends, I gave the chicks a little grain when I had some to spare, and in a few short months, they grew into sturdy roosters.

ODETTE: One day, we saw Jeanne heading for the marketplace. She was walking along the road with a basket on her head. Long tail feathers drooped over the sides of the basket.

Macmillan/McGraw-Hill

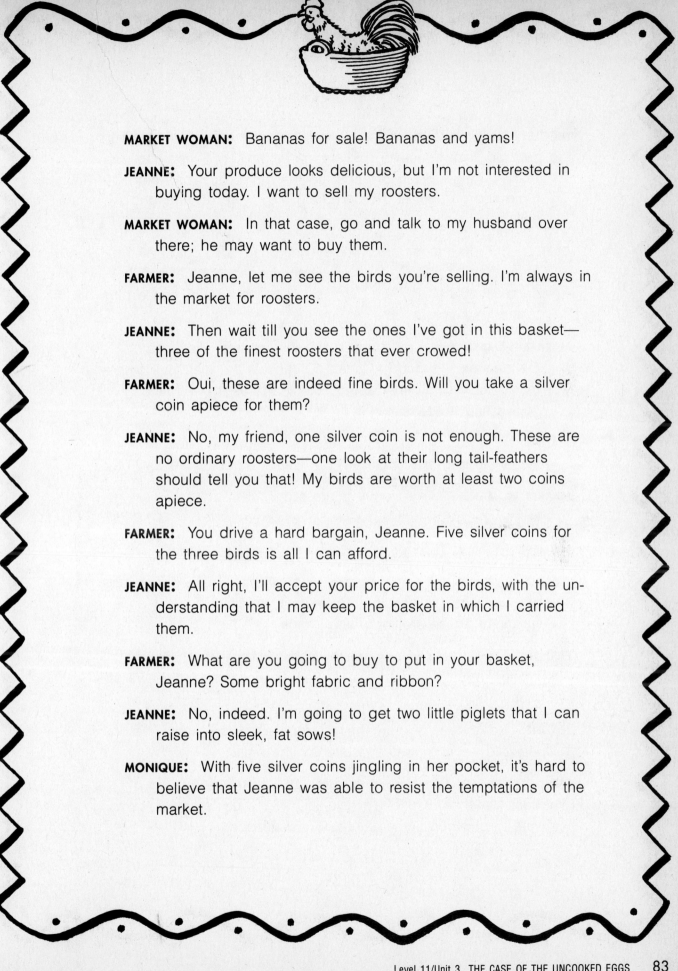

MARKET WOMAN: Bananas for sale! Bananas and yams!

JEANNE: Your produce looks delicious, but I'm not interested in buying today. I want to sell my roosters.

MARKET WOMAN: In that case, go and talk to my husband over there; he may want to buy them.

FARMER: Jeanne, let me see the birds you're selling. I'm always in the market for roosters.

JEANNE: Then wait till you see the ones I've got in this basket—three of the finest roosters that ever crowed!

FARMER: Oui, these are indeed fine birds. Will you take a silver coin apiece for them?

JEANNE: No, my friend, one silver coin is not enough. These are no ordinary roosters—one look at their long tail-feathers should tell you that! My birds are worth at least two coins apiece.

FARMER: You drive a hard bargain, Jeanne. Five silver coins for the three birds is all I can afford.

JEANNE: All right, I'll accept your price for the birds, with the understanding that I may keep the basket in which I carried them.

FARMER: What are you going to buy to put in your basket, Jeanne? Some bright fabric and ribbon?

JEANNE: No, indeed. I'm going to get two little piglets that I can raise into sleek, fat sows!

MONIQUE: With five silver coins jingling in her pocket, it's hard to believe that Jeanne was able to resist the temptations of the market.

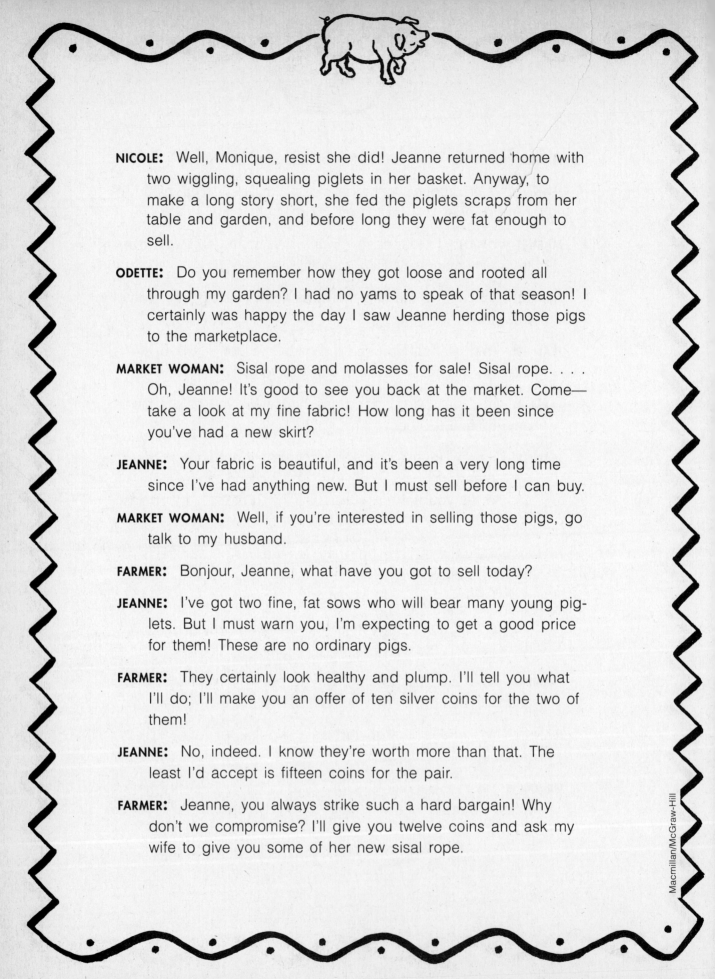

NICOLE: Well, Monique, resist she did! Jeanne returned home with two wiggling, squealing piglets in her basket. Anyway, to make a long story short, she fed the piglets scraps from her table and garden, and before long they were fat enough to sell.

ODETTE: Do you remember how they got loose and rooted all through my garden? I had no yams to speak of that season! I certainly was happy the day I saw Jeanne herding those pigs to the marketplace.

MARKET WOMAN: Sisal rope and molasses for sale! Sisal rope. . . . Oh, Jeanne! It's good to see you back at the market. Come— take a look at my fine fabric! How long has it been since you've had a new skirt?

JEANNE: Your fabric is beautiful, and it's been a very long time since I've had anything new. But I must sell before I can buy.

MARKET WOMAN: Well, if you're interested in selling those pigs, go talk to my husband.

FARMER: Bonjour, Jeanne, what have you got to sell today?

JEANNE: I've got two fine, fat sows who will bear many young piglets. But I must warn you, I'm expecting to get a good price for them! These are no ordinary pigs.

FARMER: They certainly look healthy and plump. I'll tell you what I'll do; I'll make you an offer of ten silver coins for the two of them!

JEANNE: No, indeed. I know they're worth more than that. The least I'd accept is fifteen coins for the pair.

FARMER: Jeanne, you always strike such a hard bargain! Why don't we compromise? I'll give you twelve coins and ask my wife to give you some of her new sisal rope.

Macmillan/McGraw-Hill

JEANNE: All right; that's a fair trade.

MONIQUE: And did Jeanne use the money to buy herself a new skirt?

NICOLE: No, indeed. Instead, she looked at every goat in the market and picked out the finest one that her twelve silver coins would purchase. That afternoon, we saw Jeanne leading her goat home on a long sisal rope. The goat gnawed on the rope as they walked along the road.

ODETTE: That goat would eat anything! It ate the sleeve of my favorite blouse that was hanging on the clothesline! See, here's the patch I had to sew.

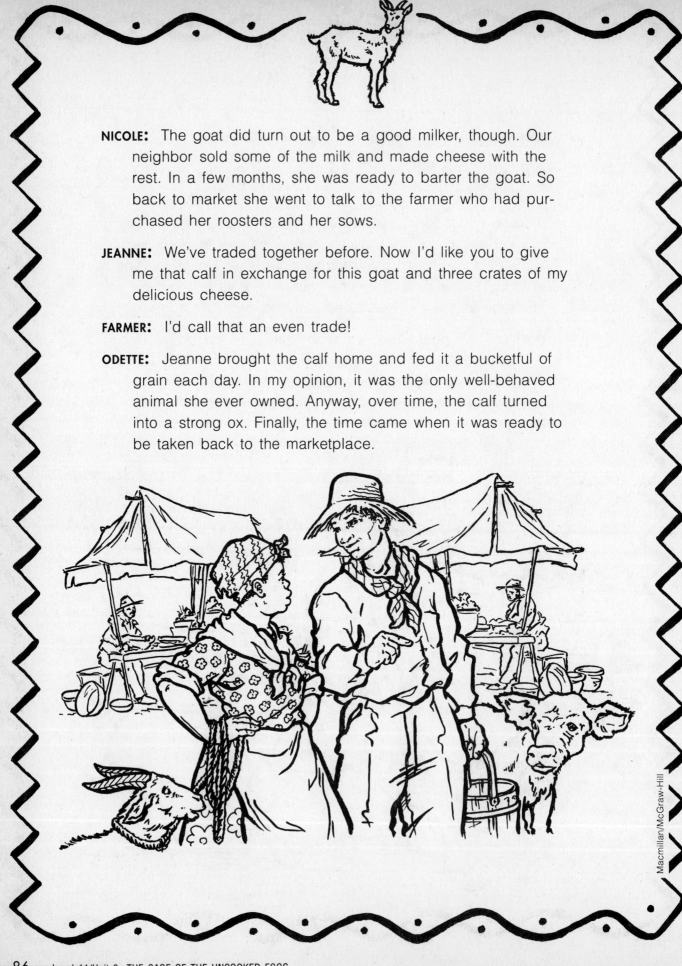

NICOLE: The goat did turn out to be a good milker, though. Our neighbor sold some of the milk and made cheese with the rest. In a few months, she was ready to barter the goat. So back to market she went to talk to the farmer who had purchased her roosters and her sows.

JEANNE: We've traded together before. Now I'd like you to give me that calf in exchange for this goat and three crates of my delicious cheese.

FARMER: I'd call that an even trade!

ODETTE: Jeanne brought the calf home and fed it a bucketful of grain each day. In my opinion, it was the only well-behaved animal she ever owned. Anyway, over time, the calf turned into a strong ox. Finally, the time came when it was ready to be taken back to the marketplace.

Macmillan/McGraw-Hill

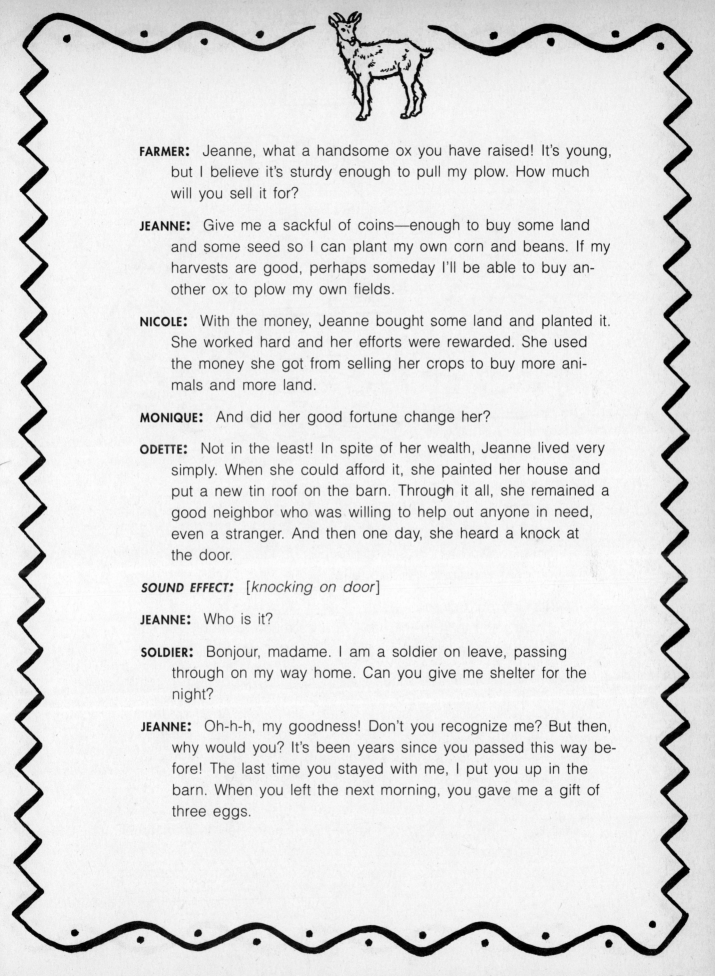

FARMER: Jeanne, what a handsome ox you have raised! It's young, but I believe it's sturdy enough to pull my plow. How much will you sell it for?

JEANNE: Give me a sackful of coins—enough to buy some land and some seed so I can plant my own corn and beans. If my harvests are good, perhaps someday I'll be able to buy another ox to plow my own fields.

NICOLE: With the money, Jeanne bought some land and planted it. She worked hard and her efforts were rewarded. She used the money she got from selling her crops to buy more animals and more land.

MONIQUE: And did her good fortune change her?

ODETTE: Not in the least! In spite of her wealth, Jeanne lived very simply. When she could afford it, she painted her house and put a new tin roof on the barn. Through it all, she remained a good neighbor who was willing to help out anyone in need, even a stranger. And then one day, she heard a knock at the door.

SOUND EFFECT: [*knocking on door*]

JEANNE: Who is it?

SOLDIER: Bonjour, madame. I am a soldier on leave, passing through on my way home. Can you give me shelter for the night?

JEANNE: Oh-h-h, my goodness! Don't you recognize me? But then, why would you? It's been years since you passed this way before! The last time you stayed with me, I put you up in the barn. When you left the next morning, you gave me a gift of three eggs.

SOLDIER: Of course, now I remember you. But this can't be the place I stopped at before! Why, it was just a shack with a tumbledown barn; this is a prosperous farm. What has brought you such good fortune?

JEANNE: My dear sir, how happy I am that you've returned. There's so much to tell you—and so much to thank you for! Let me put up a pot of beans while I tell you my story.

NICOLE: What a stroke of luck that the soldier happened to return!

ODETTE: Well, I'm not so sure I would call it luck! Anyway, Jeanne prepared a fine meal for the soldier—oxtail soup, chicken, fried bananas, rice and beans, and coffee. When they sat down to eat, she told him what had happened to his gift of the three uncooked eggs.

JEANNE: . . . . and so now you know how I managed to turn three eggs into all this! Please, you must stay with me and let me repay you for your generous gift by offering you my hospitality.

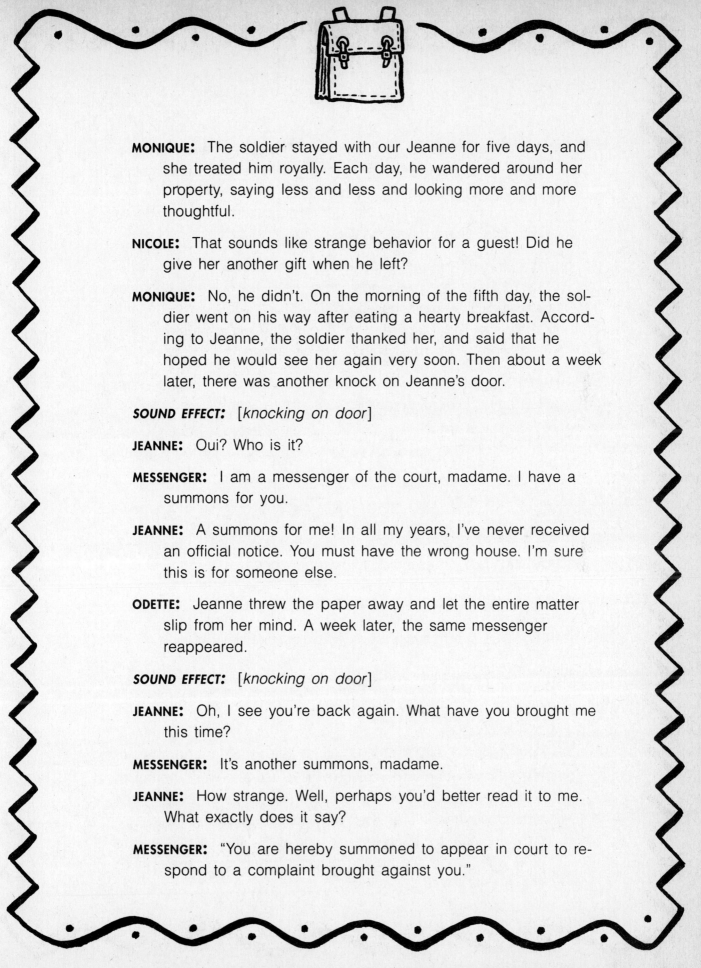

MONIQUE: The soldier stayed with our Jeanne for five days, and she treated him royally. Each day, he wandered around her property, saying less and less and looking more and more thoughtful.

NICOLE: That sounds like strange behavior for a guest! Did he give her another gift when he left?

MONIQUE: No, he didn't. On the morning of the fifth day, the soldier went on his way after eating a hearty breakfast. According to Jeanne, the soldier thanked her, and said that he hoped he would see her again very soon. Then about a week later, there was another knock on Jeanne's door.

SOUND EFFECT: [*knocking on door*]

JEANNE: Oui? Who is it?

MESSENGER: I am a messenger of the court, madame. I have a summons for you.

JEANNE: A summons for me! In all my years, I've never received an official notice. You must have the wrong house. I'm sure this is for someone else.

ODETTE: Jeanne threw the paper away and let the entire matter slip from her mind. A week later, the same messenger reappeared.

SOUND EFFECT: [*knocking on door*]

JEANNE: Oh, I see you're back again. What have you brought me this time?

MESSENGER: It's another summons, madame.

JEANNE: How strange. Well, perhaps you'd better read it to me. What exactly does it say?

MESSENGER: "You are hereby summoned to appear in court to respond to a complaint brought against you."

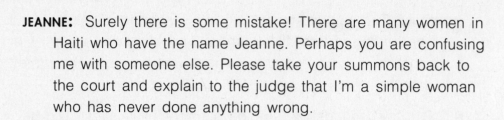

JEANNE: Surely there is some mistake! There are many women in Haiti who have the name Jeanne. Perhaps you are confusing me with someone else. Please take your summons back to the court and explain to the judge that I'm a simple woman who has never done anything wrong.

ODETTE: One day, about a week later, Jeanne was working in her fields. I saw the messenger from the court come to her house and tack the summons up on the door. At this point, Jeanne knew she could ignore it no longer. She put on a clean dress and went to ask the village schoolteacher for his advice.

JEANNE: Schoolteacher, what should I do? I know I haven't committed any crimes. I'm not the woman they want!

SCHOOLTEACHER: Well, Madame Jeanne, this may be a case of mistaken identity, but I don't think you should ignore this summons. It says, "Failure to respond to this summons may result in imprisonment."

JEANNE: Oh, dear! What shall I do? That sounds serious.

SCHOOLTEACHER: It *is* serious. My nephew once got a summons to appear in court, and when he didn't show up, they came and took him away!

JEANNE: Oui, I've heard of such dreadful things happening.

SCHOOLTEACHER: My advice to you is to go to the courthouse in Port-au-Prince. You must settle this matter before someone comes to arrest you!

NICOLE: So, what did Jeanne do?

ODETTE: What anyone in her place would do. She woke before the rooster crowed, put on her good dress, and tied a new scarf around her head. Then, carrying her shoes on her head so they wouldn't get dusty on the long walk, she set off to Port-au-Prince. When she arrived at the courthouse, the first person she saw was the soldier!

NICOLE: The soldier? But what was he doing there? I thought he was going home on leave?

MONIQUE: Ah, just wait until you hear! The clerk directed Jeanne to take a seat on a bench across from the soldier. Then the judge called for order in the court.

SOUND EFFECT: [*gavel banging*]

JUDGE: The court will now hear The Case of the Uncooked Eggs. Will the party who is bringing suit please step forward and identify himself?

SOLDIER: I am bringing this suit, Judge.

JUDGE: Against whom is your suit directed?

SOLDIER: Against that woman who is sitting on the bench across from me.

JUDGE: State the nature of your complaint.

SOLDIER: Several years ago, I gave this woman a gift, and, because of my generosity, she is a wealthy woman today. I am here to get what I feel is rightfully mine—a share of her riches.

MONIQUE: What a nerve! I can't believe the soldier actually said that!

NICOLE: Neither could Jeanne!

JUDGE: We will now hear from the accused. Please come forward.

JEANNE: Your honored Judge, I cannot understand why this soldier is suing me, for I've taken nothing that is his. In fact, I *gave* him food and shelter!

JUDGE: Is this true, soldier?

SOLDIER: I once asked this woman for a night's shelter. She gave me a bite to eat and allowed me to sleep in her barn. To show my thanks, I gave her a gift of three eggs.

JUDGE: And why does that now entitle you to share this woman's wealth?

SOLDIER: When I met this woman, she had barely enough beans for an evening meal. Today she has flocks of chickens and a pasture filled with goats and cows. She has fields of corn, beans, and carrots, not to mention a garden of beautiful roses! She's a rich woman—all because of the eggs I gave her. It is only fair that she share her wealth with me!

JUDGE: Madame, how do you respond to this?

JEANNE: Well, Your Honor, the soldier did *not* give me my animals, my land, or my money. He gave me only three eggs! Everything that I have today, I earned through my own hard work.

MONIQUE: Oui, Jeanne spoke the truth—what's right is right! Surely you'll tell me that the judge dismissed the case?

ODETTE: Alas for our poor friend Jeanne, he did not.

JUDGE: This is indeed a complicated case that will have to be properly tried. I, therefore, order you both to have lawyers prepare arguments to present in court. This case is adjourned for two weeks.

NICOLE: And so, Jeanne hired a lawyer to defend her. Two weeks later, she and the soldier both reappeared in court with their lawyers.

ODETTE: But this time, according to what Jeanne told us, the soldier's story sounded very different.

SOUND EFFECT: [*gavel banging*]

JUDGE: This court is now in session. The court will hear The Case of the Uncooked Eggs. The lawyer for the soldier may speak first.

LAWYER 1: Merci, Your Honor. I call my client to the witness stand to tell us how he first met this woman.

SOLDIER: Well, sir, a few years ago, I asked this woman for a night's shelter. She fed me a few burned beans for dinner and gave me a bed of wet straw under her leaky barn roof. However, having a generous nature, I rewarded her with a bountiful gift of three large eggs.

LAWYER 1: And did this stingy woman appreciate your gift?

LAWYER 2: Your Honor, I object! There is nothing to indicate that my client is stingy! In fact, my evidence will show that her generosity is well known.

JUDGE: Objection sustained. Proceed.

LAWYER 1: Well, then, what happened when you saw this woman again?

SOLDIER: I learned that it was *my* gift that had led to her wealth! Imagine my surprise! It was clear that I deserved more than just her gratitude.

LAWYER 1: And what do you feel would be fair payment for starting this woman on the road to riches?

SOLDIER: I only seek what is just—nothing more. I would accept half her land and livestock, for without my gift she would still be poor.

JUDGE: You may step down. The court will now hear from the lawyer for the accused.

LAWYER 2: Your Honor, though my client was very poor, she treated the soldier with generosity. In return, he gave her a gift—a gift that she could use in any way she saw fit. It was her hard work, not the eggs, that brought her wealth. I now call my client to speak on her own behalf.

ODETTE: And so, it was Jeanne's turn to tell her story.

MONIQUE: Finally! And then the judge ruled in her favor, oui?

NICOLE: No! The case went on and on as the two lawyers argued. At last, on Friday afternoon, the judge said he would announce his decision the following Monday.

ODETTE: That evening, after Jeanne had returned home, I stopped by her house to see how she was feeling.

JEANNE: Oh, my friend, I am exhausted! If someone were to drop a handkerchief on me, I would fall to the floor! I am almost willing to divide my property with the soldier rather than face that courtroom another day.

ODETTE: I begged her not to lose heart; after all, the trial was almost over. As we spoke, a stranger appeared at the door.

POOR MAN: Excuse me, madame. Will you offer charity to a poor man? Can you spare a little something for me to eat?

JEANNE: Please go away! I'm not giving out charity today, for tomorrow I may have nothing!

POOR MAN: I'm sorry to hear that. What's troubling you so, if I may ask?

ODETTE: Well, Jeanne told the poor man her story. By the time she finished, she had relented about turning him away. You see, it was not in her nature to be unkind.

JEANNE: Ah, well, my troubles aren't your fault. Come in and let me find some rice and beans for your supper.

POOR MAN: Merci, madame. Perhaps I can repay your kindness with some advice. Eat well on Saturday and Sunday. Get up early Monday morning, make yourself coffee, and walk to the city. I will be waiting for you in the courtroom.

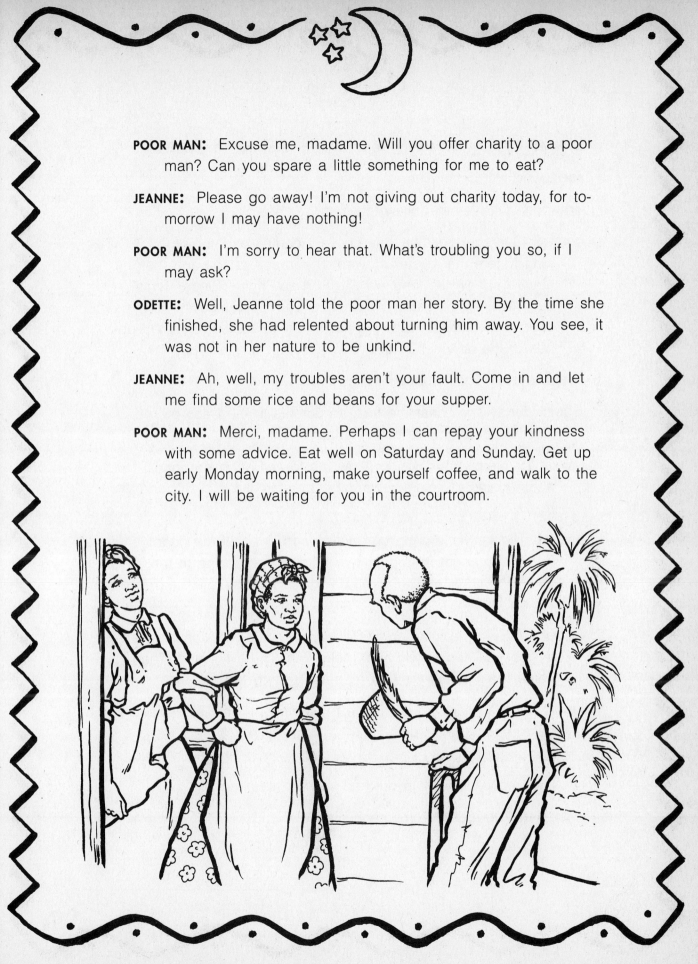

JEANNE: *You* will be waiting for me? But what can you do?

POOR MAN: You shall see.

MONIQUE: Did Jeanne follow the man's advice?

ODETTE: Oui, she did. She was up very early Monday morning, long before the rooster crowed. She made coffee and then started out on the long walk to Port-au-Prince. Since it was such an important day, Nicole and I accompanied her to court. When we arrived, the poor man was already seated on one of the benches in the rear.

SOUND EFFECT: [*gavel banging*]

JUDGE: Today I will hear the final arguments in the Case of The Uncooked Eggs. The soldier's lawyer will begin.

LAWYER 1: Merci, Your Honor. Allow me to call attention once again to the most praiseworthy character of my client, and to his . . .

ODETTE: The lawyer droned on and on and on. Half the people in the courtroom, including the judge, were dozing in the heat. The other half were watching the flies buzz around the ceiling fan.

NICOLE: When at last the soldier's lawyer concluded, Jeanne's lawyer spoke—and spoke and spoke. Finally, he finished. Then came the moment we had all been waiting for!

JUDGE: I have heard the evidence presented by both sides, and I have reached a verdict.

ODETTE: From his bench in the back of the courtroom, the poor man stood up, calling out and waving his cane.

POOR MAN: Judge! One moment, please!

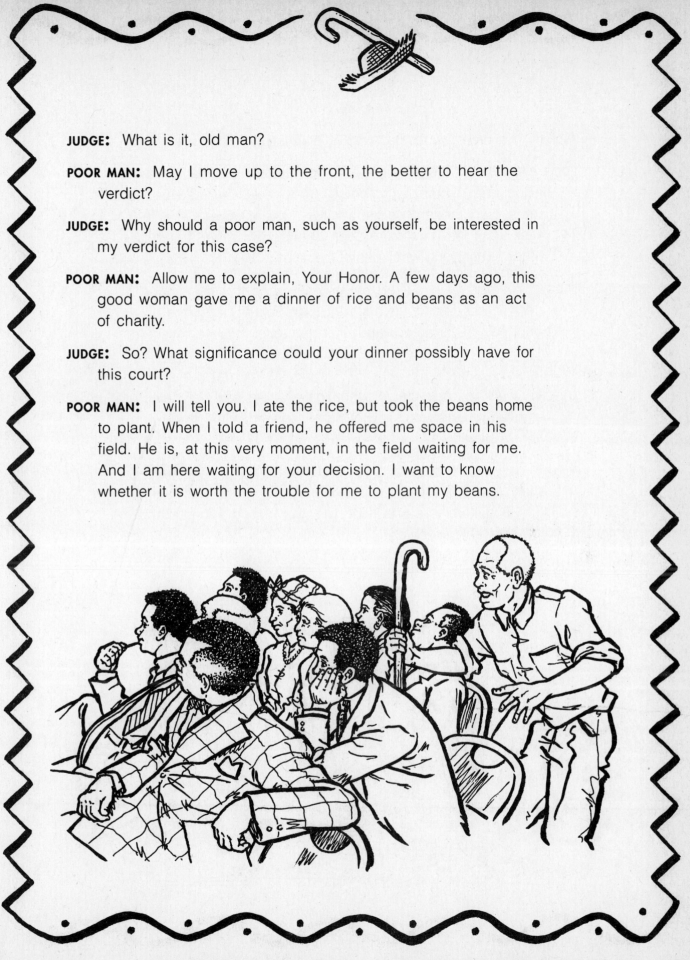

JUDGE: What is it, old man?

POOR MAN: May I move up to the front, the better to hear the verdict?

JUDGE: Why should a poor man, such as yourself, be interested in my verdict for this case?

POOR MAN: Allow me to explain, Your Honor. A few days ago, this good woman gave me a dinner of rice and beans as an act of charity.

JUDGE: So? What significance could your dinner possibly have for this court?

POOR MAN: I will tell you. I ate the rice, but took the beans home to plant. When I told a friend, he offered me space in his field. He is, at this very moment, in the field waiting for me. And I am here waiting for your decision. I want to know whether it is worth the trouble for me to plant my beans.

JUDGE: Old man, whoever heard of planting cooked beans?

POOR MAN: Well, Judge, this good woman told me that it was believed in court that eggs could produce flowers and pigs and goats. So I thought perhaps I, too, should make the effort. After all, if the laws have been changed and eggs can give all that, just think what beans can do!

JUDGE: Hmmm. . . . Your statement has made this case quite clear to me. The court rules that the soldier's claim is unfounded, unwarranted, and unreasonable. Case dismissed!

MONIQUE: So Jeanne won! Bravo!

ODETTE: Oui! The next day, Jeanne gave a big party to celebrate. And the guest of honor was none other than the poor man whose cleverness had won the case for her.

NICOLE: All the neighbors came, and what a feast there was—goat stew, chicken and chili, saffron rice, fruit, and cakes galore. But there was one thing missing from the menu, and can you guess what it was?

ALL: EGGS!

Macmillan/McGraw-Hill

BLOCKING DIAGRAM

Arrange eight chairs and two benches, as shown.

1. NICOLE	6. SOLDIER	11. BUS DRIVER
2. MONIQUE	7. MESSENGER	12. FARMER
3. ODETTE	8. LAWYER 1	13. MARKET WOMAN
4. POOR MAN	9. LAWYER 2	14. SCHOOLTEACHER
5. JEANNE	10. JUDGE	

COSTUME SUGGESTIONS

Jeanne, Nicole, Monique, Odette, and Market Woman The performers reading the parts of women can wear brightly colored skirts and blouses. Print scarves wrapped around the head and tied on top or in back will complete their costumes.

The Soldier This character can wear a pair of tan pants and a tan or dark-colored shirt.

Bus Driver, Farmer, Messenger, Schoolteacher, and Poor Man Light-colored, short-sleeved shirts, pants, and straw hats make effective costumes for the men. The poor man's clothing should look more worn than that of the others.

Judge The performer reading the part of the judge can dress in a long black robe with a white scarf wound and looped at the neck.

Lawyers The lawyers can wear shirts and ties with jackets and dark pants.

Pronunciation Guide

au revoir (ô rəv wä′) — good-bye
bonjour (bən zhu̇r′) — good day
madame (ma dam′) — form of address for a woman
merci (mâr sē′) — thank you
oui (wē) — yes
Petionville (pā′ shôn vēl′) — name of a town
s'il vous plaît (sē′ vü plā) — if you please

Macmillan/McGraw-Hill

Dog Gone
By Robert Sim

name: Patches

description: small, cute, with spots

disappeared: Sunday night

Contact: Marty King

telephone: 555-6942

Reward!

CAST
NARRATOR
MARTY KING
FRAN ALLOY
HENRY ALLOY
PATCHES 1
PATCHES 2
JENNIFER ALLOY
CINDY
MR. LOPEZ

Macmillan/McGraw-Hill

NARRATOR: It was a beautiful day for a wedding. The bride and groom, Fran and Henry, had been planning to marry for some time, but they wanted to give their children time to become comfortable with the idea. You see, Fran and Henry were married once before—to other people, I mean—and each had a child. Henry's daughter, Jennifer, was living with her mother in a distant city. Fran's son, Marty, was closer at hand. In fact, he was just about to escort his mother down the aisle.

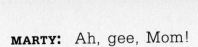

MARTY: Ah, gee, Mom!

FRAN ALLOY: Marty, all I said was that you look very hand-some in your tuxedo.

MARTY: Come on, Mom, I look like a waiter.

HENRY ALLOY: Only until your mom pins this rose on your lapel; then you'll look very important.

MARTY: You mean, on top of everything else, I have to wear flowers?

FRAN ALLOY: Just one.

MARTY: I'll smell like a girl. Is Henry wearing one?

HENRY ALLOY: You bet. What kind of stepdad would I be if I let you sport a rose solo?

MARTY: Well, I guess it's okay then.

HENRY ALLOY: Sure it is! Besides, as soon as we get back to my house—excuse me, I mean *our* house—we'll change out of these fancy duds and shoot some hoops. What do you say?

MARTY: I wish I was shooting hoops now.

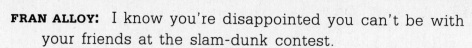

FRAN ALLOY: I know you're disappointed you can't be with your friends at the slam-dunk contest.

MARTY: It's okay, Mom. I know you want me to be here.

HENRY ALLOY: Uh-oh, look at the time. Can't keep the guests waiting.

FRAN ALLOY: Henry, are you sure you have the ring?

HENRY ALLOY: I do. I mean, sure I'm sure. That is, I think I have it. Just a minute, let me check . . .

NARRATOR: Despite Henry's sudden attack of nerves, the wedding went smoothly, and the reception was lots of fun. Afterward, Marty, Fran, and Henry filled a doggie bag for Marty's favorite pooch:
> Name—Patches
> Occupation—family pet
> Duties—lie around, chew slippers,
>   bark at mail-carrier, and so on.

HENRY ALLOY: I'd take it easy on the wedding cake, if I were you, Marty. My guess is that Patches would really prefer these little Vienna sausages.

FRAN ALLOY: Do you have enough space for a couple of spoonfuls of chopped liver? Just the thing to top off those sausages!

MARTY: Mom, I've got enough here to last Patches a week. I don't want him to get fat, you know!

NARRATOR: Patches's main job, though, was being Marty's best friend. That was especially true ever since Marty had moved out of his old neighborhood and away from Jake and Chris, his other best friends. Now that it was summer, Marty needed somebody to chase, wrestle, and generally horse, uh, dog around with on lazy afternoons in his new neighborhood.

Macmillan/McGraw-Hill

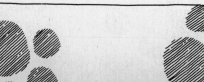

MARTY: C'mon, Patches, ol' boy! Want to play catch?

PATCHES 1: Woof.

PATCHES 2: Translated that means, "Watch the ol' boy stuff, but okay."

NARRATOR: A few weeks after the wedding, everyone began to settle in and feel more at home, especially Marty. One evening before dinner, Henry asked Marty if he wanted to go outside and play one-on-one. While they were taking a break, Henry decided to bring up an important subject.

HENRY ALLOY: Say, Marty, can we talk for a minute?

MARTY: Sure. What's up?

HENRY ALLOY: I want you to know that I really think you've done a great job adjusting to a new house, a new neighborhood, and a new family setup. I know having to deal with all these changes hasn't been easy. You probably really miss your friends, right?

MARTY: Yeah. I liked hanging out with them.

HENRY ALLOY: Have you made any friends around here yet?

MARTY: No, not really. A lot of the kids are away at camp and on vacation and stuff.

HENRY ALLOY: Well, I think I've got an idea that just might improve your situation. You know my daughter, Jennifer? Well, she grew up in this house.

MARTY: Yeah, Mom told me. She said I'm in Jennifer's old room; that's why everything was pink when I moved in.

HENRY ALLOY: Didn't take us long to change that, did it?

MARTY: One whole weekend, I think.

HENRY ALLOY: That's what I remember, too. But listen, Marty. What I want to tell you is that Jennifer called last night. She's planning to visit us for a few weeks. I just wanted to let you know.

MARTY: It's okay with me. I don't care if she comes or not.

HENRY ALLOY: It doesn't sound like you're exactly thrilled with the prospect.

MARTY: Well, she's a girl.

HENRY ALLOY: She's also a few years older than you, but let me explain why I think it's a good idea. First, you and Jennifer are brother and sister now. It would be good for you to get to know one another. Does that make sense?

MARTY: Sort of.

HENRY ALLOY: And, it will give Mom a chance to know Jennifer the way I know you. That's important, too, don't you think?

MARTY: I guess.

HENRY ALLOY: And finally, as I mentioned, Jennifer grew up in this neighborhood. She knows practically everybody. I'm sure she could introduce you to some kids your own age. It couldn't hurt, right? . . . You're not saying anything.

MARTY: When's she coming?

Macmillan/McGraw-Hill

HENRY ALLOY: She's flying in on Sunday afternoon. Will you help make her feel welcome?

MARTY: Yeah. Is that all?

HENRY ALLOY: Yup, that's it. I think you two are really going to hit it off. Well . . . I guess I'll go in and help Mom get dinner started. Hey, Patches, be a good boy now and look after Marty.

PATCHES 1: Woof.

PATCHES 2: For humans, that means, "Of course I will; that's my job!"

NARRATOR: The next couple of days were pretty hectic around the house.

MARTY: Patches, it looks like the Queen of England is coming instead of Jennifer. The rugs got shampooed. Mom got shampooed.

PATCHES 1: Woof!

PATCHES 2: Translated that means, "Even *I* got shampooed!"

MARTY: At least I don't have to put on a tuxedo.

NARRATOR: Finally, Sunday arrived. Henry went to the airport and returned with Jennifer.

HENRY ALLOY: Hi, everybody, we're back! Jennifer, this is Fran.

FRAN ALLOY: It's nice to meet you, Jennifer. Your father's told me so much about you. I hope we'll become good friends.

JENNIFER: Thank you. It feels so good to be home again.

HENRY ALLOY: Jennifer, this is Marty.

JENNIFER: Hi! Oh, what a cute dog! What's your dog's name, Marty?

MARTY: Patches.

JENNIFER: Well, hello, Patches. How handsome you are! Would you like a cookie? I've got one left over from lunch on the plane.

PATCHES 1: Woof! Woof!

PATCHES 2: Yes! Yes! What else would you expect a dog to say?

Macmillan/McGraw-Hill

MARTY: He can't have it now, not until after supper.

JENNIFER: It's really small. I'm sure one little cookie wouldn't spoil his appetite.

PATCHES 1: Woof! Woof!

PATCHES 2: Marty, come on! She's right! She's right!

MARTY: I said no!

JENNIFER: Okay. Okay. You don't have to bite my head off.

FRAN ALLOY: Marty, what's gotten into you? Jennifer's just trying to be nice! I think you owe her an apology.

MARTY: Sorry.

HENRY ALLOY: Well, let's bring your bags in from the car, Jen. You'll probably want to change your clothes before dinner.

JENNIFER: Thanks, Dad. I would.

NARRATOR: Henry and Jennifer returned with her bags, which were stowed in the den. Fran checked the cinnamon rolls baking in the oven. Their sweet aroma signaled that dinnertime was near. Patches also turned up in the kitchen, finding some floor space at Jennifer's feet. Only Marty chose not to join the group, deciding instead to retreat to his room, where he pointedly closed the door. But he wasn't the only one who was uncomfortable. From the look on Jennifer's face, it was clear that she was not happy about having to sleep in the den.

HENRY ALLOY: Jennifer, as I explained in the car, we had to give Marty your old room. I know this isn't easy for you, but we couldn't put him in the cellar.

JENNIFER: No, of course not, but that's my room. It's always been my room. It's not my fault I had to move out.

HENRY ALLOY: I don't think this is about somebody being at fault, Jennifer.

FRAN ALLOY: Henry . . . Jennifer, I feel a little awkward about saying this. I know it's not a good idea for me to step between you, but I also know that neither one of you wants this visit to begin with so much tension. Perhaps I can talk Marty into camping out in the den for a while.

HENRY ALLOY: No, Fran, thank you, but it would be unfair to Marty to throw him out of his room. It's not what we worked out when we agreed to invite Jennifer.

JENNIFER: You asked his permission?

HENRY ALLOY: No, honey, listen. . . .

JENNIFER: Now I can see who the *real* stepchild in this family is.

HENRY ALLOY: Jennifer! Don't say things like that . . .

FRAN ALLOY: [*interrupting*] Jennifer, why don't the two of us go in the den for a few minutes so I can help you unpack. We won't worry about dinner for the time being. Your father will watch it. He's already stirred up everything else!

HENRY ALLOY: Fran, I . . . oh, brother.

NARRATOR: Unfortunately, things didn't improve much during dinner. Marty mashed his peas to a fine pulp, Henry and Jennifer stewed, and Fran served the meal in an unhappy silence. Only the shrill ring of the telephone broke the gloom.

FRAN ALLOY: Hello. . . . Yes, she is. Just a moment please, and I'll get her. Jennifer, it's Cindy.

JENNIFER: Hi, Cindy! Yeah . . . a couple of hours ago. Uh . . . okay. I can't really talk about it now; I'll tell you later. . . . Hold on, I'll ask. Dad and Fran, would it be okay if Cindy came over after we finish dinner?

FRAN ALLOY: Of course she can.

JENNIFER: Cindy, the answer is yes! . . . Oh. Unh-unh. No. . . . She's cool. That's *not* the problem. I'll tell you later. . . . Who? Put her on. . . . Lisa! How are you? . . . I know. I miss you, too. . . . Sure. Hold on, I'll ask. Dad, can Lisa come, too?

HENRY ALLOY: Sure. Invite the whole school. They can sleep in the living room.

JENNIFER: Great! Hey, Lisa, my dad says I can invite everybody, and they can sleep over!

HENRY ALLOY: Wait a minute, Jennifer! I was just kidding.

JENNIFER: Okay. I'll see you later.

HENRY ALLOY: Jennifer, I didn't mean . . .

FRAN ALLOY: Henry, while Jennifer's upstairs getting ready, why don't you and I get these dishes done and prepare some snacks for the girls?

HENRY ALLOY: But . . .

FRAN ALLOY: Jennifer, you may be excused. Marty, do you want to help?

MARTY: No way. It's her party. I'm going outside.

HENRY ALLOY: Take Patches with you, but don't let him out of the backyard. He's still having trouble dealing with all the traffic on this street compared to your old neighborhood.

MARTY: Don't worry, I'll be careful. Hey, Patches, where are you? Want to go outside? Patches? Where are you?

FRAN ALLOY: I think Patches is upstairs with Jennifer, Marty.

MARTY: Crazy dog! What are you doing upstairs with her?

PATCHES 1: Woof.

PATCHES 2: For your information, I was looking for that cookie I was promised.

MARTY: C'mon, Patches! We're going outside. . . . C'mon I said! Okay, Patches, stay inside! See if I care.

FRAN ALLOY: Remember, Marty, stay in the backyard.

MARTY: Yes, Mom.

HENRY ALLOY: I don't get it, Fran. We planned a quiet evening at home for the four of us, and now, all of a sudden, it's turned into a teenage slumber party! We should have stopped this when the whole thing started getting out of hand.

FRAN ALLOY: But Henry, seeing her friends is very important to Jennifer. She's having a hard time coming home to so much change. Besides, by having a slumber party, we avoid the bedroom issue for at least one night.

HENRY ALLOY: True. Maybe by tomorrow, you'll think of some brilliant arrangement to get me off the hook for the next few weeks!

FRAN ALLOY: I'll do my best, Henry, but don't count on it!

HENRY ALLOY: Is that the doorbell? It hasn't even been ten minutes! Jennifer, I think your friends are here.

JENNIFER: Thanks, Dad. I'll be right down.

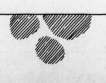

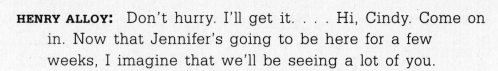

HENRY ALLOY: Don't hurry. I'll get it. . . . Hi, Cindy. Come on in. Now that Jennifer's going to be here for a few weeks, I imagine that we'll be seeing a lot of you.

CINDY: I hope so, Mr. Alloy. It's nice to see you again. Is Jen around?

HENRY ALLOY: She'll be right down. . . . Jennifer, Cindy's here.

JENNIFER: Hi, Cin!

CINDY: Jennifer!

JENNIFER: Where's Lisa?

CINDY: She went home to get her stuff. By the way, she called Donna, who called Sue, who called Maryanne. And you know what that means. If you want word to get around, telephone, telegraph . . .

JENNIFER: . . . tell Maryanne. C'mon in. I've got so much to tell you. Let's go into the living room.

CINDY: Great. Hey, I brought over my newest CDs.

HENRY ALLOY: I'll make popcorn.

JENNIFER: Dad!

HENRY ALLOY: Then I'll bow out, I promise. Say, Fran, how's the popcorn supply? Do I need to go to the store?

FRAN ALLOY: That's okay, Henry. I'm sure we've got everything that the girls will need. Why don't you come out in the kitchen and help me?

JENNIFER: Don't worry, Cindy, I'm pretty sure Dad and Fran will leave us alone. Anyway, I couldn't really talk about it on the phone, but things have been sort of weird since I got here.

CINDY: Weird? What's the matter? Is your stepmother giving you a hard time?

JENNIFER: No. Actually, she's pretty nice. It's my dad. He picked me up at the airport, and everything was fine until he told me that he'd given my bedroom to my stepbrother, Marty.

CINDY: You've got to be kidding! How could your own dad do something like that?

JENNIFER: I wish I knew. Prepare yourself, here comes the twerp now! What do you want, Marty?

MARTY: I want to play a tape.

JENNIFER: The Warlocks? No way. I hate heavy metal.

MARTY: I can play a tape if I want.

JENNIFER: No you can't. Now please get out of here. I'm having a party.

MARTY: Why don't *you* get out of here? Why don't you go back where you came from?

JENNIFER: For your information, I came from right here. This was my house first, you know!

MARTY: Not anymore, it isn't.

FRAN ALLOY: Hey, what's going on in here?

MARTY: She won't let me play a tape.

FRAN ALLOY: Hi. You must be Cindy.

CINDY: Oh, hi, Mrs. Alloy. It's nice to meet you.

FRAN ALLOY: Marty, Jennifer wants to visit with her friends.

MARTY: I'm not stopping her. I just want to watch TV.

FRAN ALLOY: Well, Marty, this isn't a good time to watch TV.

MARTY: What's going on around here? She shows up and I can't do anything. I can't listen to music. I can't watch TV. I can't do anything!

FRAN ALLOY: Marty, there's a lot you can do. Why don't you find something in your room to keep you occupied.

MARTY: Good idea. I think I'll just go up to *my* room and close the door.

FRAN ALLOY: Marty!

JENNIFER: You see what I mean, Cindy?

CINDY: Yeah. How juvenile can you get?

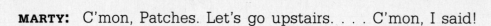

MARTY: C'mon, Patches. Let's go upstairs. . . . C'mon, I said!

FRAN ALLOY: It looks as if Patches wants to stay down here, Marty.

JENNIFER: [*baby talk to the dog*] Yeah, he doesn't like rude people.

FRAN ALLOY: Jennifer . . . oh, there's the doorbell again. I'll get it. Would one of you please grab Patches's collar? We don't want him to get out.

MARTY: If he gets out, he might run away because he doesn't know the neighborhood, so you'd better be careful.

JENNIFER: Don't worry, I'll be careful. Hey, Lisa, is that you?

NARRATOR: During the next half-hour, more of Jennifer's old friends arrived. They laughed and danced and told stories about school and boys and each other. Fran and Henry shuttled snacks in and out, while Marty played in his room with a model spaceship he built from scratch. He soared down from deep space and dropped bombs on the planet Jennifer. No one knew for certain when it happened, but sometime between the first hello and the last sleepy giggle, Patches slipped out the door and disappeared. It wasn't until the next morning that Fran discovered the dog was missing.

FRAN ALLOY: Jennifer, Henry and I have to go to work. I've already called the police and the dog pound to be on the lookout for Patches. I'll check in with you about noon to see if he's been found. I'm afraid you'll have to be the one to tell Marty that Patches is gone.

JENNIFER: Okay. I'm not looking forward to it, but I'll tell him as soon as he wakes up.

NARRATOR: As Jennifer suspected, telling Marty was not a pleasant task.

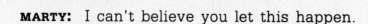

MARTY: I can't believe you let this happen.

JENNIFER: It was an accident. It's not like I did it on purpose.

MARTY: You promised you'd be careful. You promised!

JENNIFER: Marty, I'm sorry. I truly am. I'm going to look for him right now. I told all my friends, and they're all going to look for him, too. I don't know what else I can do. I really liked Patches, too, you know.

MARTY: What do you mean, you *liked* him? You're talking like Patches is dead. He's not dead. I know he's not.

JENNIFER: Marty, where are you going?

MARTY: I'm going to look for Patches, where else?

JENNIFER: But you don't know the neighborhood. I do. It's better if you stay home in case the police call or he comes back. I'll look for him.

MARTY: No way. He knows my voice. He'd never come to you.

JENNIFER: Maybe we should go together then.

MARTY: Forget it. Why don't you go look with your friends?

NARRATOR: On this sour note, Jennifer and Marty set out to begin the search. Jennifer walked down one side of the street, and Marty walked down the other. While not admitting it, each knew the other was right. Jennifer was familiar with the neighborhood and all the likely hiding places for a runaway dog. But it was Marty's voice that Patches would recognize and respond to. So, without any agreement between them, the two tried to stay together and yet apart at the same time.

MARTY: Patches! Here boy! C'mon Patches!

JENNIFER: Patches! Want a cookie? Patches! It's cookie-time!

NARRATOR: When they reached the end of the block, Jennifer turned left, and Marty turned right. It seemed as if they would go their separate ways after all. An elderly neighbor, Mr. Lopez, watched them from a chair on his porch. At his feet were two bowls, one containing water and the other small pieces of a well-done hamburger. Mr. Lopez smiled as he called across the street.

MR. LOPEZ: Is that my friend Jennifer? No, it can't be. Sounds like her, though!

Macmillan/McGraw-Hill

JENNIFER: Hi, Mr. Lopez. It's nice to see you again. How are you feeling?

MR. LOPEZ: Fine. I'm just fine. How about yourself?

JENNIFER: Not so good right now. I did a really dumb thing, Mr. Lopez. I let my stepbrother's dog escape last night. It was an accident. Honest!

MR. LOPEZ: I believe you. Is that young man over there your stepbrother?

JENNIFER: Yes, it is, and he's not too happy with me right now.

MARTY: You can say that again!

JENNIFER: See what I mean?

MR. LOPEZ: Well, call him over here. Maybe I can cheer him up.

JENNIFER: I doubt it, but you could try. Hey, Marty, come here. There's someone I want you to meet.

MARTY: I don't have time, Jennifer. I'm looking for a lost dog, in case you forgot!

MR. LOPEZ: Tell him that I have a tail for him.

JENNIFER: Marty, come here. Mr. Lopez wants to tell you something.

MR. LOPEZ: Say my tail also has four paws and a wet nose.

JENNIFER: Marty! Hurry up!

MARTY: Relax, Jennifer. What's the matter?

JENNIFER: Mr. Lopez, this is my stepbrother, Marty. Marty, this is Mr. Lopez.

MARTY: Hi, Mr. Lopez. Sorry if I seemed rude. I'm looking for my dog. You see, my new stepsister let him run away!

JENNIFER: I didn't let him! I told you it was an accident!

MARTY: Accident or not, it's still your fault!

MR. LOPEZ: You young folks sure are steamed up. Why don't you each take a deep breath and calm yourselves down. It just so happens I've got a new tenant in a fur coat living right here under this porch.

JENNIFER: You mean . . . ?

MARTY: Patches!

NARRATOR: Jennifer and Marty raced down the wooden steps and scurried to either end of the porch. Through the darkness they could see each other, but the sunlight didn't penetrate the cool space beneath the planking. If Patches was there, they couldn't tell by looking.

MARTY: Patches, are you there? Here, boy!

JENNIFER: [*making kissing noises*] Here, Patches.

MARTY: Don't do that. He hates that!

JENNIFER: He does? How do you know?

MARTY: He's a boy dog. He has to hate it. Patches! Here, boy.

JENNIFER: Over here! C'mon, Patches!

PATCHES 1: Woof! Woof!

PATCHES 2: Can't you stop shouting? I had a terrible night!

MARTY: Oh, Patches! That's you, all right!

MR. LOPEZ: Is that your dog, young man?

MARTY: Yes, sir, I'd know that bark anywhere. Thank you for finding him for me.

MR. LOPEZ: No need to thank me. Your dog found me. By the sound of things, he probably was looking for some peace and quiet. For that, he came to right place.

JENNIFER: How will we get him out from under your porch?

MARTY: Patches, if you come out, I'll let you chew my slippers.

PATCHES 1: Woof.

PATCHES 2: In other words, "Something tells me that you obviously haven't seen them lately!"

JENNIFER: Patches! [*making kissing noises*] Patches! If you come out, I'll give you a bubble bath.

PATCHES 1: Woof. Woof.

PATCHES 2: Loosely translated that means, "What do you take me for, a poodle?"

MARTY: [*loudly*] Patches!

JENNIFER: [*louder*] Patches!!

MARTY: [*louder yet*] Patches!!!

MR. LOPEZ: Hey, hey! Simmer down! You're not going to get him out by yelling and screaming.

JENNIFER: But what can we do, Mr. Lopez? He won't come out. Nothing seems to work.

MR. LOPEZ: What you haven't tried is working together. Why, look at the two of you! Jennifer, you're at one end of the porch and, Marty, you're down at the other. No wonder the poor dog is confused.

PATCHES 1: Woof.

PATCHES 2: In other words, "He's absolutely right. I'm confused."

MARTY: Jennifer, why don't you go home?

JENNIFER: Why don't you?

MR. LOPEZ: Now, both of you come over here and sit down and listen. I want to tell you a little story. I mean it now. . . . Just leave that dog in peace for a few minutes and stop arguing.

MARTY: Sorry, Mr. Lopez.

JENNIFER: I guess we were getting a little out of control.

MR. LOPEZ: You said it! Now sit quietly and listen. When I was a boy, my brother and I lived in a small village outside of Ponce, in Puerto Rico. One day, we got a special present from our uncle. It was a kite—a beautifully painted kite in the shape of a giant bird.

JENNIFER: That sounds neat.

Macmillan/McGraw-Hill

MARTY: If I had a kite, I'd fly it all day.

MR. LOPEZ: That's exactly what my brother and I wanted to do, Marty. But there was one problem—we had only one kite, and both of us wanted it.

MARTY: So, what did you do?

JENNIFER: Did you take turns?

MR. LOPEZ: No, I wish we had. Instead, we argued over who would fly the kite first. We argued about everything in those days!

MARTY: What happened then? Did one of you give in?

MR. LOPEZ: No, we began to fight. My brother pulled one way, and of course, I pulled the other way. The crazier the kite flew, the more my brother and I fought for it. Finally, the kite crashed. It was ruined.

MARTY: Did you get another one?

MR. LOPEZ: No, we never did. We couldn't tell our uncle that his wonderful gift was torn and broken because of our argument. He would have been very disappointed in us.

JENNIFER: That's too bad.

MR. LOPEZ: Yes, it was. You see, we never got another kite, and we never really got to enjoy the one we had. Jennifer, it seems to me that you and Marty are fighting over Patches, just like my brother and I fought over that kite.

JENNIFER: Yeah . . . I think you may be right, Mr. Lopez. Probably the unhappiest one around here right now is poor Patches.

MARTY: He doesn't know which one of us to listen to . . .

JENNIFER: . . . or where to turn.

MR. LOPEZ: I think Patches must feel a little like that kite being yanked around in different directions. What you two need to do is to work together.

JENNIFER: How can we, Mr. Lopez? We really don't look at things in the same way.

MARTY: She's right, Mr. Lopez. We don't.

MR. LOPEZ: Well, you might start by considering the feelings of others. Try to get along for the sake of Patches or your parents. The rest will take care of itself. For starters, why don't each of you grab one of these bowls. There's nothing like a night under a porch to make a dog hungry and thirsty.

MARTY: Okay, Mr. Lopez.

MR. LOPEZ: Stay together this time. Try calling him from the same side of the porch.

JENNIFER: Here, Patches. Are you thirsty? I've got a bowl of cool water! C'mon boy!

MARTY: Patches, how about some burgers? Are you hungry?

PATCHES 1: Woof! Woof!

PATCHES 2: In case you couldn't guess, I said, "Give me a break! Of course I'm hungry!"

MARTY/JENNIFER: Come here, Patches!

PATCHES 1: Woof. Woof.

PATCHES 2: In human terms that means, "I'm out of here!"

NARRATOR: With Patches safely rescued from under Mr. Lopez's porch, Marty and Jennifer turned to go.

MARTY: Thanks for letting Patches stay under your porch, Mr. Lopez. You're a dog's best friend. C'mon, Patches, let's go home.

MR. LOPEZ: That's okay, Marty. Despite the circumstances, I'm glad I had a chance to meet you.

JENNIFER: Thanks for everything, Mr. Lopez. If it's all right, I'd like to stop in and see you again during my visit.

MR. LOPEZ: Any time, Jennifer, any time. You're welcome to come by, too, Marty.

MARTY: Thanks, Mr. Lopez.

JENNIFER: Marty, I'm going to look for my friends. I want them to know that Patches is okay.

MARTY: Tell them I said thanks for helping, Jennifer, I really mean it. Patches says thanks, too. On second thought, if you don't mind, maybe we'll come along with you and thank them in person.

JENNIFER: Good idea, Marty. Besides, that way I can introduce you to Lisa's brother, who's about your age. He's got a dog, too.

PATCHES 1: Woof!

PATCHES 2: No translation necessary!

BLOCKING DIAGRAM

Arrange seven chairs and a stool, as shown. The narrator can use a music stand to hold the script.

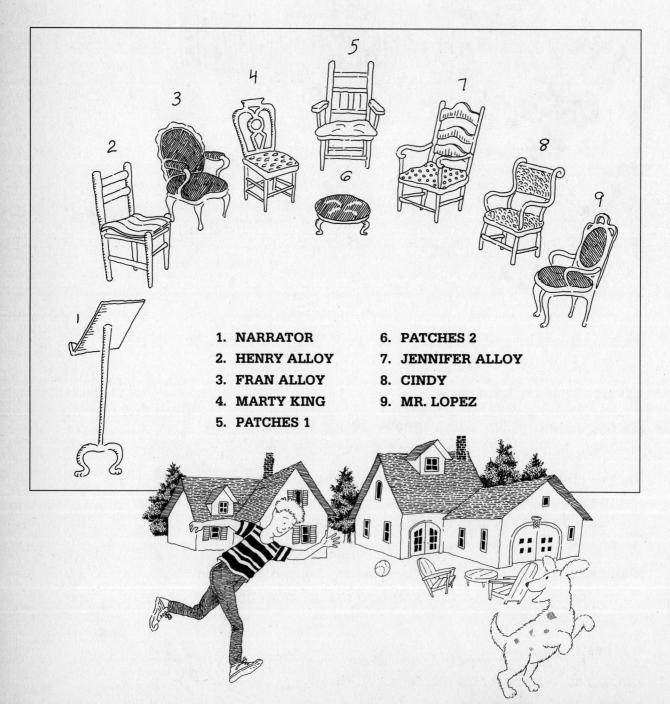

1. **NARRATOR**
2. **HENRY ALLOY**
3. **FRAN ALLOY**
4. **MARTY KING**
5. **PATCHES 1**
6. **PATCHES 2**
7. **JENNIFER ALLOY**
8. **CINDY**
9. **MR. LOPEZ**

The World.

PRICE FIVE CENTS   NEW YORK   PRICE FIVE CENTS

'Round the World with Nellie Bly

by Claire Daniel Chapelle

PRICE FIVE CENTS

The Cast

CAST

- NEWSBOY
- NARRATOR
- MR. GODDARD
- NELLIE BLY
- MR. CHAMBERS
- PASSENGER 1
- YOUNG GIRL
- RANDOLPH CHARLES
- JULES VERNE
- MADAME VERNE
- DRIVER

- TELEGRAPH OPERATOR
- IRENE SARLES
- MR. SARLES
- ENGINEER
- TICKET AGENT
- MR. FUHRMANN
- JAPANESE REPORTER
- CHIEF ALLEN
- PASSENGER 2
- JOHN JENNINGS
- DOCTOR

NEWSBOY: EXTRA! EXTRA! Read all about it! Get the latest edition of the *World* hot off the press!

NARRATOR: Back in the year 1888, people relied on newspapers to fill them in on all the news, for television and radio had not yet been invented. Almost every city had several competing newspapers, and nowhere was the competition more fierce than in New York City. The *Tribune*, the *Sun*, the *Times*, and the *World*, to name just a few of the papers, used every gimmick they could think of to attract readers. The *World*, a newspaper owned by Joseph Pulitzer, had the largest circulation of all, due in part to the articles of a talented young woman reporter named Nellie Bly. Nellie was always on the lookout for a sensational story idea to present to her editor, Mr. Goddard.

Macmillan/McGraw-Hill

MR. GODDARD: Good morning, Nellie. Well, you look a little bleary-eyed this morning. Have you given any thought to this week's stories?

NELLIE BLY: Morning, Mr. Goddard. I can imagine that I do look a little tired. You see, I stayed up all night doing nothing but thinking about possible stories, and I only managed to come up with one idea.

MR. GODDARD: You were up all night, and you only have one idea? Nellie, that doesn't sound like you!

NELLIE BLY: Yes, but this idea isn't like most, Mr. Goddard. You see, I want to go around the world!

MR. GODDARD: Nellie, a trip around the world isn't a news story. People do that all the time.

NELLIE BLY: The way I plan to do it *will* be a news story. I'll go around the world like Phileas Fogg, the hero in Jules Verne's book *Around the World in Eighty Days*. But the gimmick is that I'll beat Fogg's record and make the trip in seventy-five days! I know it'll work, Mr. Goddard. I stopped at a steamship office before coming to work this morning, and I've calculated that it will take me precisely 75 days and 4 hours!

MR. GODDARD: Well, Nellie, it's a good idea, but not a new one. I'm sorry to disappoint you, but the *World* has been kicking that notion around for quite a while. In fact, we got so far as deciding to send John Jennings.

NELLIE BLY: Oh. . . . Well, Mr. Jennings is an excellent reporter, but just think how much more sensational it would be if a woman made the trip! We'd sell many more newspapers!

MR. GODDARD: I don't think there's anything I can do at this point, Nellie. You see, Mr. Chambers has already made the decision; but if you'd like, we can go talk to him.

NELLIE BLY: Absolutely! Let's see him now! I'm sure he can be convinced to change his mind.

MR. GODDARD: Well, Nellie, if anyone can do it, you're the one!

NARRATOR: Mr. Goddard spoke from experience! You see, in 1888, few women worked outside the home, and for those who did, good jobs were hard to come by. Nellie Bly was one of the first female newspaper reporters, so she was used to hearing the opinion that a woman couldn't do what a man could. Determined to disprove that notion, Nellie Bly approached Julius Chambers, managing editor of the *World*, and described her idea.

MR. CHAMBERS: I don't think it's a good idea. I know you can do whatever you set your mind to, Nellie. But the fact that you're a woman complicates everything.

NELLIE BLY: I've carried out much harder assignments, Mr. Chambers. Remember the time I disguised myself and worked side by side with the women in the box factory to expose dangerous working conditions?

MR. GODDARD: She's right, Chambers. And who could forget the ten days Nellie spent on Blackwell's Island posing as a mentally ill woman so she could report on conditions inside an insane asylum? Thanks to her articles, changes are being made.

Macmillan/McGraw-Hill

NELLIE BLY: And I've been in the most dangerous sections of New York and Pittsburgh. And travel isn't new to me; I went to Mexico . . .

MR. CHAMBERS: Accompanied by your mother . . .

NELLIE BLY: But *I* had to take care of *her*!

MR. GODDARD: Nellie, even Jules Verne's hero Phileas Fogg was accompanied by a servant. You'd need a companion.

NELLIE BLY: I'm not an Englishman who sits sipping tea while being waited on by servants. This is 1888, and I'm an American woman!

MR. CHAMBERS: Exactly my point! Women don't travel alone, American or not.

NELLIE BLY: Now just a minute! When I investigated the insane asylum, you let me go alone. I was hungry and cold and scared, but I survived to write about it. You owe me the chance to do this! And you know in your heart that I am the best person to go!

MR. CHAMBERS: But what about baggage? With all the belongings a woman has to take, it would slow you down. Besides, you don't speak any foreign languages. I know you're excited about the idea, but there's no point in discussing it further. Only a man could do this!

NELLIE BLY: Very well. Send John Jennings if you want. I'll start the very same day for some other newspaper, and I'll beat him!

MR. CHAMBERS: Nellie, I believe you would.

NARRATOR: Both men looked at each other. It didn't take long for them to make up their minds.

MR. CHAMBERS: All right. If anyone goes, it will be you, Nellie. I promise.

NARRATOR: Almost a year passed without any more discussion of Nellie's idea. Then, one cold November evening, Mr. Chambers asked Nellie to step into his office.

MR. CHAMBERS: Can you be ready to start around the world the day after tomorrow?

NELLIE BLY: I can start today!

MR. GODDARD: Nellie, we know you're resourceful, but how can you be ready so soon?

NELLIE BLY: Phileas Fogg took an hour to pack, but I know I can beat his record! After all, I've had almost a year to plan!

MR. GODDARD: So, what will you take?

NELLIE BLY: I'll take one small gripsack with a blouse, two caps, a blazer, and three veils to protect my face from the sun and wind. I'll also include pens and pencils, paper, pins, needles and thread, a dressing gown, slippers, toilet articles, underwear, handkerchiefs, and if I can fit it in, a jar of cold cream. I'll wear a two-piece dress and an overcoat and carry a silk raincoat.

MR. GODDARD: There, Chambers, what did I tell you? Do you still think her baggage will be a problem?

NARRATOR: On Thursday, November 14, 1889, Nellie arrived at the pier in Hoboken, New Jersey. The twenty-four-hour clock that would record her time was set, and Nellie boarded the steamship *Augusta Victoria*. At precisely 9:40 in the morning, the whistle blew and the steamship pulled away from the pier.

NEWSBOY: EXTRA! EXTRA! Read all about it! Nellie Bly to make an unequaled, rapid-transit, record-breaking trip around the globe! Read all about it in the latest edition of the *World*!

NARRATOR: On her way at last, Nellie leaned over the rail to wave at the crowd of well-wishers.

NELLIE BLY: Good-bye! Don't worry! It's only a matter of 28,000 miles, and 75 days and 4 hours until I shall be back again! Think of me as having a wonderful vacation and the most enjoyable time of my life.

PASSENGER 1:   My goodness, you've got quite a crowd to see you off!

NELLIE BLY: Yes, I certainly do. In addition to my mother and a few friends, my editors and other business associates came down to the pier. You see, I'm attempting to beat Phileas Fogg's record and report on it for my paper, the *World*.

PASSENGER 1: Well, we certainly have a great day for sailing.

NELLIE BLY: We do? As a matter of fact, the sea seems a bit choppy to me. Oooh! . . . Excuse me, I'm not feeling too well!

PASSENGER 1: Ha! And she thinks she's going around the world!

NARRATOR: Miserable with seasickness, Nellie went to her cabin and slept until 4:00 the next afternoon. When she awoke, she found that she had gotten her "sea legs," and every trace of seasickness was gone. It didn't take long for word to get around the ship about Nellie's trip. One young girl waited for an opportunity to talk with Nellie.

YOUNG GIRL: Ma'am, are you really going around the world?

NELLIE BLY: Why, yes, I am.

YOUNG GIRL: I told my mother I wanted to go around the world, but she said girls don't do things like that.

Macmillan/McGraw-Hill

NELLIE BLY: She's right, usually they don't. But I'm trying to change people's attitudes, so we girls can do what we want to do.

YOUNG GIRL: I think you're a brave lady. I want to be like you when I grow up.

NARRATOR: Eight days later, on November 22nd, the *Augusta Victoria* docked in Southampton, England, at 2:30 in the morning. Despite the hour, Nellie was on deck with her gripsack in hand. She watched as a tall young man stepped off the tug that had nudged the ship into the pier.

MR. CHARLES: Miss Bly? Miss Nellie Bly? I'm Randolph Charles, the London correspondent for the *World*. Is your baggage ready? Shall I call a porter?

NELLIE BLY: This one bag is all I have, Mr. Charles.

MR. CHARLES: It is? Then let's get you checked through customs. I've an important message for you from Monsieur and Madame Jules Verne. They've invited you to stop and see them.

NELLIE BLY: The Vernes! How wonderful! I'd love to meet them, but it's not on my route. Is it possible to make a detour?

MR. CHARLES: I think it can be done *if* you are willing to go without sleep for two days.

NELLIE BLY: Sleep? I'd give up any amount of sleep to meet Jules Verne!

MR. CHARLES: There is one other factor, Miss Bly. You must be clear about the risk. By changing your itinerary, you could ruin your schedule.

NELLIE BLY: I think we should try it! I can't think of anyone I would like to meet more than Jules Verne! His character, Phileas Fogg, is the reason I'm here today. I think it's worth the risk; besides, my readers will love it! Think of all the newspapers we'll sell!

NARRATOR: So Nellie and Mr. Charles traveled by train to London and then to Dover. From there, they took a boat across the English Channel to France and caught a train to Amiens. Late that day, a tired but thrilled Nellie Bly arrived at the Vernes' beautiful estate. With Mr. Charles acting as translator, Nellie and the Vernes were able to carry on a conversation.

JULES VERNE: Mademoiselle Bly, you are so young! You're almost a child!

MME. VERNE: But she is a remarkable young woman.

NELLIE BLY: Thank you, madame. I would like to thank you for the kind invitation to visit your home.

JULES VERNE: The pleasure is ours, dear lady. As a writer, I invent my characters. It's not often I meet someone such as you who has a life as interesting as a character in one of my books.

MME. VERNE: I'm curious, mademoiselle. How did you get the name Nellie Bly? It's not your real name, is it?

NELLIE BLY: No, my real name is Elizabeth Cochrane, but American reporters often use pen names. After I finished my first news article, we were trying to think of a catchy name for me. Just then a reporter walked by humming an old Stephen Foster tune called "Nelly Bly," and I thought to myself, "That's the name for me! Nellie Bly!"

MME. VERNE: I admire you American women. You're so modern.

NELLIE BLY: There's nothing so modern as your husband's novels. As one of your most avid readers, Mr. Verne, there's something I've always been curious about. How did you get the idea for *Around the World in Eighty Days?*

JULES VERNE: Well, Mademoiselle Bly, you'll be happy to learn that I got the idea from reading a newspaper. One morning I saw an article that said a journey around the world might be done in eighty days. Suddenly, a great idea for a story

Macmillan/McGraw-Hill

occurred to me! Suppose the main character was trying to prove that such a journey might be made. As you know, when we travel from west to east, we gain a day. Well, what would happen if the main character forgot all about the international dateline? He would think that he'd failed—only to find out at the last minute that he had succeeded after all! The idea worked, and the book turned out rather well. Now, tell me, how did you get the idea to try *my* idea?

NELLIE BLY: About a year ago, I was up all night racking my brains for story ideas for my paper. When I couldn't think of anything new or different, I finally said to myself, "I might as well be halfway around the world!" Then I looked over at my bureau and saw your book. So I said to myself, "Why not? Why can't *I* do that?"

JULES VERNE: And how do you plan to go?

NELLIE BLY: I plan to follow Phileas Fogg's route most of the way. From here, I'll go to Calais on the French coast, and then on to Brindisi, Italy. From Italy, I'll travel to Port Said, Ismailia, and Suez, all in Egypt. Then I'll go to Aden in Yemen, then Colombo, Ceylon. My last stops will include Penang, the island of Singapore, the British colony of Hong Kong, and Yokohama in Japan. Finally, I'll sail to San Francisco and take a train across the United States back to New Jersey—all in less time than it took your hero, Mr. Verne!

JULES VERNE: If you do it in seventy-nine days or less, I shall applaud you with both hands.

MME. VERNE: It is almost time for your train, my dear. We thank you very much for coming to see us.

NELLIE BLY: Merci! Even if I don't complete the trip in time, it's been worth it just to meet you! Au revoir!

NARRATOR: The readers of the *World* seemed to think it was worth it, too, as they eagerly read Nellie's account.

NEWSBOY: EXTRA! EXTRA! Read all about it! Nellie Bly meets famous author Jules Verne! Only in today's *World*!

NARRATOR: From Amiens, Nellie Bly took the train to Calais. There she parted from Mr. Charles and caught yet another train for the two-day trip to Brindisi in southern Italy. On the train, Nellie wrote in her journal.

NELLIE BLY: Today, November 24, 1889, is the tenth day of my journey around the world. I have sixty-five days left. The side trip to Amiens to meet the Vernes has occasioned no delay. We are only an hour or two behind schedule.

NARRATOR: The train arrived in Brindisi at 1:30 in the morning of the eleventh day of Nellie's trip. A large omnibus met the passengers and carried them down to the pier. Nellie found her cabin on the steamship *Victoria*, which was bound for Colombo, Ceylon. After stowing her bag, Nellie rushed back to the deck to find the omnibus driver.

NELLIE BLY: Excuse me, sir, can you tell me if there is a telegraph office nearby? Would I have time to send a cable before we sail?

DRIVER: Yes, miss, there is a telegraph office that is not far from the pier. The streets are too narrow for my omnibus, but we can walk there. Since the ship is not due to sail for almost an hour, you can probably make it, if we hurry.

NELLIE BLY: Hurrying is second nature to me. Let's go!

NARRATOR: The driver rushed Nellie down the gangplank and through several dark and winding streets.

DRIVER: Ah, here we are!

NELLIE BLY: But the telegraph office is closed; there's no one here! My cable will have to wait until I reach the next port.

DRIVER: Here it is customary to ring the night bell to awaken the operator. See, he's coming now. I'll translate for you, if you'd like.

NELLIE BLY: Thank you very much. Please tell him that I'm sorry to wake him, but I need to send a cable to New York.

Macmillan/McGraw-Hill

TELEGRAPH OPERATOR: New York? Where is that, young lady?

NELLIE BLY: Why, it's the biggest city in North America! Does he mean to say he's never heard of New York?

TELEGRAPH OPERATOR: I've heard of York, England. Are you sure you have the name right? Perhaps you mean Yorkshire?

NELLIE BLY: No, indeed. I mean New York City in the state of New York in the United States of America.

TELEGRAPH OPERATOR: One moment, please. I must find it first. Then I'll have to determine the cost. We don't send many cables to America. This will take some time.

NARRATOR: The telegraph operator took out several large books and began to search through them for the information he needed.

NELLIE BLY: Please ask him to hurry! The boat leaves in fifteen minutes!

TELEGRAPH OPERATOR: Ah, yes, here it is. New York, New York, in the United States. You were right, young lady! Do you have your message and the money? Good. I'll send this cable right away.

NARRATOR: Just then a shrill whistle sounded.

NELLIE BLY: My ship! It's leaving without me!

DRIVER: Can you run? Let's try to make it!

NARRATOR: Nellie Bly ran as fast as she could and reached the pier in time to see a steamship pulling away. But to her great relief, she discovered that it was another liner. Her ship, the *Victoria*, was still tied up! Meanwhile, back home, people eagerly reached for the newspapers to find out about Nellie Bly's progress.

NEWSBOY: EXTRA! EXTRA! Read all about it! Nellie Bly steams through the Suez Canal!

NARRATOR: Such was the topic of discussion at the breakfast table at the Sarles home in Rye, New York.

IRENE SARLES: Has the *World* come today, Father? May I see it?

MR. SARLES: Since when did you start to read the newspaper, young lady?

IRENE SARLES: Since Nellie Bly started her trip around the world! She's been gone for twenty-four days. Haven't you been reading about it?

MR. SARLES: I read *The New York Times*, not the *World*! So who, may I ask, is Nellie Bly?

IRENE SARLES: Oh, Father! She's the woman who reports on conditions in factories and mental institutions for the *World*. Now she's trying to circle the globe in less time than Phileas Fogg.

MR. SARLES: That's a foolish stunt! She'll never make it!

IRENE SARLES: She's already made it across Europe and as far as Port Said. Now she's writing about her trip through the Suez Canal. Why, in this account, she describes how they dress for dinner and dine on board the ship, and how they spend their evenings on deck. She even tells about having dishwater poured on her one morning when her porthole was open!

MR. SARLES: Goodness! That sounds positively dreadful!

IRENE SARLES: But she makes everything seem so interesting! Do you know it's so hot at night that the men sleep on the deck? And listen to this! She describes the camel markets, Egyptian women in black veils, and boys diving from the banks of the canal for silver coins. According to her itinerary, she should be in Colombo, Ceylon, by now. Oh, what a trip!

NARRATOR: Nellie Bly was, indeed, in Colombo. And four days later, on December 12th, Nellie Bly was *still* in Colombo, cabling her reports back to New York and waiting impatiently

Macmillan/McGraw-Hill

for her ship to leave for China. Finally, the day of departure came, and Nellie boarded the *Oriental*. There she met the chief engineer strolling on the deck.

ENGINEER: Good morning! It's a lovely day for sailing, isn't it?

NELLIE BLY: It will be when we set sail. Do you know when that will be?

ENGINEER: We can't sail until the *Nepaul* comes in. She was to have been here at daybreak, but she's a slow old boat.

NELLIE BLY: But we're behind schedule! I've been waiting to leave for days!

ENGINEER: Well, at least Colombo is a pleasant place to visit. I hope you've had an opportunity to do some sightseeing. By any chance, did you ride in the rickshaws and visit the Buddhist temples and enjoy the wonderful Chinese food?

NELLIE BLY: Yes, I did all that, and I even saw a snake-charmer with a cobra. But waiting is difficult for me. You see, I'm traveling around the world for my paper, and I'm trying to do it in seventy-five days. This is day twenty-nine, and I've got only forty-six more days to get back home!

ENGINEER: I see! Like Phileas Fogg! But since there's absolutely nothing you can do about the delay, you should try to relax and enjoy yourself.

NELLIE BLY: I do apologize for seeming so out-of-sorts. I fear my patience has given out, due to the long delay. But you see, I have nightmares of creeping back to New York ten days behind schedule . . . a failure.

NARRATOR: At that precise moment, Nellie spotted a thin line of blue smoke just above the horizon.

NELLIE BLY: Look! Do you see that smoke off in the distance. It looks like a steamship!

ENGINEER: I believe it's the *Nepaul*! As soon as she docks and her passengers are brought aboard, we'll sail.

NARRATOR: On December 16th, the *Oriental* anchored at Penang off the coast of Malaysia. Nellie Bly continued to cable her reports back to New York.

MR. CHAMBERS: What do we have from Nellie today, Goddard?

MR. GODDARD: It's good copy. She describes the Chinese places of worship in Penang where she drank tea with the priests. They couldn't say a word to each other, so they just smiled.

MR. CHAMBERS: It's hard to imagine Nellie not saying anything!

MR. GODDARD: Oh my goodness, just listen to this! She bought a monkey.

MR. CHAMBERS: A what?

MR. GODDARD: A monkey! In Singapore, she saw some monkeys and decided she had to have one, so she bought one. It's impossible to predict what Nellie will do next!

MR. CHAMBERS: Well, I know what *we'll* do. We'll print it. It'll make good copy—readers will love it! By the way, can't we think of something to get even more readers interested in Nellie?

MR. GODDARD: How about a contest of some sort? . . . Yes! A contest to predict when Nellie will make it back.

MR. CHAMBERS: Brilliant! It'll get all New York involved! Everyone will want to keep track of Nellie's journey, and the only way they'll be able to do that is by reading the *World*!

NEWSBOY: EXTRA! EXTRA! Read all about it! Enter the Nellie Bly Guessing Match! Get your coupon in this issue of the *World*!

NARRATOR: Meanwhile, on the way from Singapore to Hong Kong, Nellie's ship encountered a monsoon. Rains fell and wild winds rocked the boat. Nellie's cramped cabin was flooded. Despite the monsoon, Nellie reached Hong Kong on the morning of December 23rd—two days early! She immediately made her way to a ticket office and eagerly approached the agent.

NELLIE BLY: Good morning. Can you please tell me the date of the first sailing for Japan?

TICKET AGENT: Excuse me, but are you Nellie Bly? We've been looking for a woman by that name traveling alone from Singapore.

NELLIE BLY: Why, yes, I'm Nellie Bly. You must have heard about my trip. I'm ahead of schedule! Isn't that wonderful?

TICKET AGENT: Miss Bly, I'm afraid I have bad news for you. You're going to be beaten.

NELLIE BLY: How can that be? I've made up for the five days I lost in Colombo, unless . . . unless the boat to Japan has sunk!

TICKET AGENT: The steamship hasn't sunk, but you are going to lose.

NELLIE BLY: Lose? I don't understand. What do you mean?

TICKET AGENT: Aren't you having a race around the world?

NELLIE BLY: Of course! I'm running a race with time!

TICKET AGENT: Time? I don't think that's her name. The other woman . . .

NELLIE BLY: *Her* name? The other woman? What *are* you talking about?

TICKET AGENT: Don't you know? The day you left New York, another woman named Elizabeth Bisland started out in the opposite direction. She's trying to beat you, and it looks as if she's going to do it. She has thousands of dollars to pay ships to leave early. Do you have that kind of money?

NELLIE BLY: No, of course not!

TICKET AGENT: Well, she left here three days ago. Based on the scheduled sailing dates, you can't even leave Hong Kong for at least five days. And then you'll have to wait five more days in Yokohama.

NELLIE BLY: So it's impossible to catch up?

TICKET AGENT: I'm afraid so. I must say, I'm astonished you didn't know about her. I was told that your paper sent her.

NELLIE BLY: That's impossible! Mr. Chambers would never do such a thing!

NARRATOR: As Nellie and the ticket agent were speaking, a ship's officer approached the window. He was from the *Oceanic*, the ship scheduled to take Nellie to Japan and then on to San Francisco.

MR. FUHRMANN: So you're our famous passenger Nellie Bly. It's a pleasure to meet you! I recognized you from the cartoons that I saw in the newspapers we picked up in San Francisco. I couldn't help overhearing part of your conversation, and I want to say that you shouldn't worry about someone beating you around the world. This other woman is just trying to steal your idea for her magazine, the *Cosmopolitan.* Your newspaper didn't send her to race against you.

NELLIE BLY: I knew they'd never do that! You see, I promised my editor I'd go around the world in seventy-five days, and that's what I'll do. I'm not racing with anybody—except Phileas Fogg!

MR. FUHRMANN: That's the spirit!

NARRATOR: While waiting for the ship to Japan, Nellie Bly explored Hong Kong. After climbing a mountain high above the city, she wrote this entry in her journal on December 24, 1889.

NELLIE BLY:

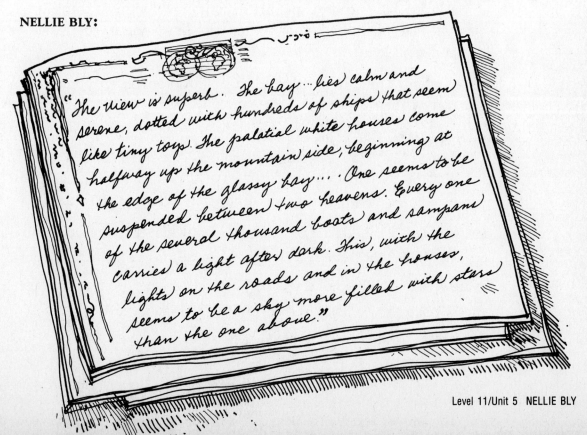

"The view is superb. The bay...lies calm and serene, dotted with hundreds of ships that seem like tiny toys. The palatial white houses come halfway up the mountain side, beginning at the edge of the glassy bay.... One seems to be suspended between two heavens. Every one of the several thousand boats and sampans carries a light after dark. This, with the lights on the roads and in the houses, seems to be a sky more filled with stars than the one above."

NARRATOR: Meanwhile, back in New York, readers eagerly awaited each edition of the *World* to track Nellie Bly's progress.

NEWSBOY: EXTRA! EXTRA! Read all about it. Nellie Bly now in Japan. World-famous globe-trotter has reached Yokohama!

IRENE SARLES: Father, did you bring home today's edition of the *World*? I'm dying to read about Nellie Bly!

MR. SARLES: Nellie Bly, Nellie Bly! That's all I hear around this house!

IRENE SARLES: Father, listen to Nellie's latest report from Yokohama; it's dated January 3rd. She says, "I arrived here today safely and in good health. . . . The commander of the *Oceanic* expects to make an extraordinary effort between here and San Francisco. . . . I hope to be in New York January 25. Happy New Year to all my friends in America." Father, I think she's going to make it!

MR. SARLES: I hope she does. But she's still got a long way to go.

IRENE SARLES: There's a coupon for a contest in the newspaper. All you have to do is predict exactly how long you think it will take Nellie to complete her trip. I'm going to cut it out and send it in!

MR. SARLES: Those newspaper editors will do anything to get you to buy their papers.

IRENE SARLES: Oh, come on, Father! The winner gets a free trip to Europe and $250 spending money! You can enter, too! I'll save you the coupon in tomorrow's paper. I predict she'll make it in exactly 72 days, 7 hours, and 4 minutes! What do you think?

MR. SARLES: I think I'd like to see that newspaper after you've finished reading it.

NARRATOR: While Nellie was in Japan, a reporter from a Japanese newspaper interviewed her about her visit.

REPORTER: Did you enjoy Japan, Miss Bly?

Macmillan/McGraw-Hill

NELLIE BLY: Oh yes! If I were married, I would tell my husband I know where Eden is, and I would bring him to Japan. Japan is beautiful. Your cities are clean, and your people are full of grace and charm.

REPORTER: What has been the most unusual thing you have seen?

NELLIE BLY: Everything is unusual. In fact, in a place like this, it's unusual for anything to be familiar! It's all strange—and quite wonderful. For example, you dress so differently! A Japanese woman wears a flowing kimono with long sleeves in which she carries her calling cards, money, combs, and hairpins. And your houses, with their sliding doors and rice-paper windows instead of glass, are nothing like the houses in America. Everything here enchants me.

REPORTER: Is there anything you would do differently if you could begin your trip all over again?

NELLIE BLY: Yes, I would bring along one of those new cameras made by George Kodak. I want to remember all that I've seen, and it would have been nice to have pictures.

NARRATOR: Two days later, on January 7th, Nellie boarded the *Oceanic* to sail to San Francisco. The ship's engineer, Chief Allen, had prepared a surprise for her.

CHIEF ALLEN: Welcome, Miss Bly! In honor of your trip, we've posted this motto above the engines. It says, "For Nellie Bly, we'll win or die."

NELLIE BLY: That's wonderful, Chief Allen! I have precisely twenty-one days left. Full steam ahead!

NARRATOR: In the New York offices of the *World*, Nellie's editors were busy planning.

MR. CHAMBERS: Goddard, here are the designs for our new Nellie Bly parlor game. We'll call it " 'Round the World with Nellie Bly."

MR. GODDARD: Great! We'll run it right after she gets back.

MR. CHAMBERS: By the way, I just received a cable saying that Nellie has left Japan. What plans have we made for her welcome in San Francisco?

MR. GODDARD: The mayor and the press club will meet her ship. As she steps ashore, a band will play "Home Sweet Home" and "Nelly Bly."

MR. CHAMBERS: Shouldn't someone from the New York office be there, too? How about Jennings?

MR. GODDARD: Good idea. Since he didn't get to make the trip around the world, the least we can do is send him to accompany Nellie on her special train home.

NARRATOR: However, out on the Pacific Ocean, the weather wasn't cooperating with Nellie's schedule. On January 9th, her

Macmillan/McGraw-Hill

third day out from Japan, a monsoon hit. The ship pitched violently in the rolling seas. News of the storm reached the New York offices of the *World* and made the headlines.

NEWSBOY: EXTRA! EXTRA! Read all about it! Will Nellie Bly survive a fierce monsoon?

NELLIE BLY: Chief Allen, I only have nineteen days left! With this storm, I don't think I'll make it back in time. If I fail, I'll be too ashamed to go back to New York.

CHIEF ALLEN: Don't talk that way, Miss Bly. We're doing everything we can. I'm running the engines harder than they've ever been run before, and the entire crew is pitching in. So, chin up and smile, Miss Bly. We're doing our very best!

NARRATOR: Unknown to Nellie, another storm in another part of the world was also threatening her trip. A blizzard, raging in the western part of the United States, was burying the rails on the transcontinental route that Nellie was to take home. Stuck in a snowdrift, someplace in the Sierra Nevada Mountains, was the train carrying reporter John Jennings, Nellie's escort home.

PASSENGER 2: Jennings, we've been snowbound here for hours. Do you have any idea where we are?

MR. JENNINGS: Well, sir, I was just talking with the conductor. He says this place is called Emigrant Gap. There must be ten feet of snow on the tracks already, and it's still coming down in flakes the size of soda crackers!

PASSENGER 2: Did the conductor say how they plan to get us out of here?

MR. JENNINGS: This train can't move until the rotary snowplows get here, but that could take days.

NARRATOR: And it did. It was several days before word of Jennings's plight reached the New York office of the *World*.

MR. GODDARD: Chambers, read this! It's a telegram from Jennings. He's snowbound in that blizzard.

MR. CHAMBERS: Let's see. . . . He says they've been stuck for fifty hours. The snow is twelve to eighteen feet deep in places, and some miners on snowshoes have brought food to the passengers. That's quite a story right there—print it!

MR. GODDARD: Right away, boss! By the way, we're busy rerouting Nellie's special train for the trip back. It's clear she won't be able to travel across the country on the northern route as we'd planned.

NARRATOR: Back at sea, the monsoon finally blew itself out, and the ship reached San Francisco on January 21st.

NEWSBOY: EXTRA! EXTRA! Read all about it! Nellie Bly's ship sighted in San Francisco harbor on day sixty-eight of her historic trip!

NARRATOR: With just seven days remaining, what could go wrong now?

MR. FUHRMANN: Attention all passengers! I regret to announce that the ship's doctor is unable to locate our health certificate. We fear it may have been left back in Yokohama. If that is the case, no one will be permitted to land until the next ship arrives from Japan!

NELLIE BLY: Then I'll just have to jump overboard and swim ashore!

NARRATOR: At that moment, the ship's doctor came running in.

DOCTOR: Fortunately, that won't be necessary, Miss Bly. I found the certificate stuck in a cubbyhole in my desk! Unfortunately, however, there is a report that we have a case of smallpox on board; everyone will have to be examined.

NELLIE BLY: How long will that take?

MR. FUHRMANN: Don't worry, Miss Bly. I've asked the doctor to examine you first.

NARRATOR: Following a quick examination, Nellie boarded a waiting tugboat that was to take her into the San Francisco harbor. As the tugboat steamed away, the doctor leaned over the ship's railing and called out.

DOCTOR: Miss Bly! Wait! Stop! I forgot to examine your tongue! You cannot land until I see it!

NELLIE BLY: All right! How's this, Doctor?

NARRATOR: With that, Nellie Bly stuck out her tongue at the doctor.

DOCTOR: Looks fine to me!

NARRATOR: After a rousing welcome home to America, Nellie's special train left San Francisco. Two hours later, the train stopped in Lathrop, California, to pick up another passenger—John Jennings.

NELLIE BLY: Mr. Jennings, what a surprise! A *World* reporter in San Francisco told me that you were trapped in a snowbound train someplace in the Sierra Nevada Mountains! How on earth did you get here, and are you all right?

MR. JENNINGS: I'm fine now, thanks, but I had to hike fourteen miles on snowshoes to get to a train that would bring me here.

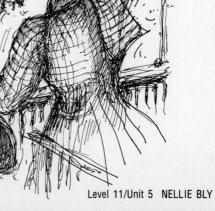

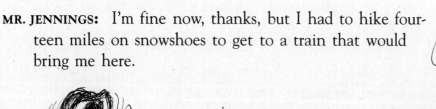

NELLIE BLY: Fourteen miles through snowdrifts! How did you find your way?

MR. JENNINGS: One of the miners served as my guide. In fact, it was his wife's snowshoes that I wore.

NELLIE BLY: You've done a brave thing. I can see why Mr. Chambers wanted to send you around the world.

MR. JENNINGS: And yet you, Miss Bly, were an even better choice. It looks like you'll make it in time.

NELLIE BLY: I haven't made it yet. Have you heard anything about the other woman—Elizabeth Bisland?

MR. JENNINGS: Not a word. She's probably in the middle of the Atlantic Ocean right now. Don't worry; you're going to make it.

NARRATOR: From there, the special train carrying Nellie Bly sped across the United States, stopping along the way so that people could see and talk to the remarkable woman. Nellie passed through Chicago and Philadelphia, and then, on January 25th—the seventy-second day of her journey—she arrived at her final destination—Jersey City.

ALL EXCEPT NELLIE BLY: Hurrah! Hurrah for Nellie Bly!

NARRATOR: The cannons in New York Harbor boomed out the news of Nellie's arrival. She took off her cap, threw it into the crowd, and then addressed her well-wishers.

NELLIE BLY: I'm so happy, and not only because I've gone around the world in seventy-two days, but because I'm home!

NARRATOR: Nellie Bly had beaten Phileas Fogg's time by nearly eight days! When the official watch was checked, 72 days, 6 hours, 11 minutes, and 14 seconds had elapsed. Elizabeth Bisland, the young woman who had tried to challenge Nellie, did not arrive until four days later. Not only had Nellie done what she set out to do, she'd also established a record that would stand for thirty-nine years. More important, she had shown the world what a determined young woman could do!

Macmillan/McGraw-Hill

Blocking Diagram

Arrange twenty chairs, as shown. The narrator and the newsboy can use music stands to hold their scripts.

1. NARRATOR	9. JOHN JENNINGS	16. TELEGRAPH OPERATOR
2. MADAME VERNE	10. MR. CHAMBERS	17. JAPANESE REPORTER
3. JULES VERNE	11. MR. GODDARD	18. CHIEF ALLEN
4. RANDOLPH CHARLES	12. NEWSBOY	19. DOCTOR
5. ENGINEER	13. PASSENGER 1	20. PASSENGER 2
6. NELLIE BLY	14. YOUNG GIRL	21. IRENE SARLES
7. TICKET AGENT	15. DRIVER	22. MR. SARLES
8. MR. FUHRMANN		

Nellie Makes the News

As this cartoon suggests, the *World* wasn't the only business that got mileage from Nellie Bly's trip.

Eager to secure more readers than the 337,367 advertised in their banner, the editors of the *World* printed a coupon for The Nellie Bly Guessing Match in each issue of the paper, beginning on December 1, 1889. Over a million readers entered the contest.

Macmillan/McGraw-Hill

Nellie Bly Parlor Game

On the day after Nellie Bly's triumphant return, the *World* printed this game on one entire page of the paper. It was so popular that it was manufactured as a board game, printed in color, and sold long after Nellie's trip had become "old news." Cut out the game, tape it together, and play "'Round the World with Nellie Bly" with your friends.

SPEEDING ACROSS THE ATLANTIC

1. The object of the game is to complete the circuit of the World and reach New York first.

2. This is a game for 2, 3, or 4 players. Each player takes a colored counter to represent a Voyager.

3. The player with the highest throw on the number cube starts, and then each player follows in turn.

4. Each player moves according to the number thrown on the cube. A play of 1 puts voyagers on the first day, a play of 2 on the second day, and so on.

5. Players must follow directions on any given day or space that they may happen to reach, i.e., "go back a day", "lose another throw." If no directions are given, they may remain on that space.

6. The directions are, however, to be followed only when a player reaches a space by a throw of the number cube. For instance, having gone back a day or moved as directed, players are to disregard the directions found at their second resting place.

7. The first player to reach New York or beyond wins the game.

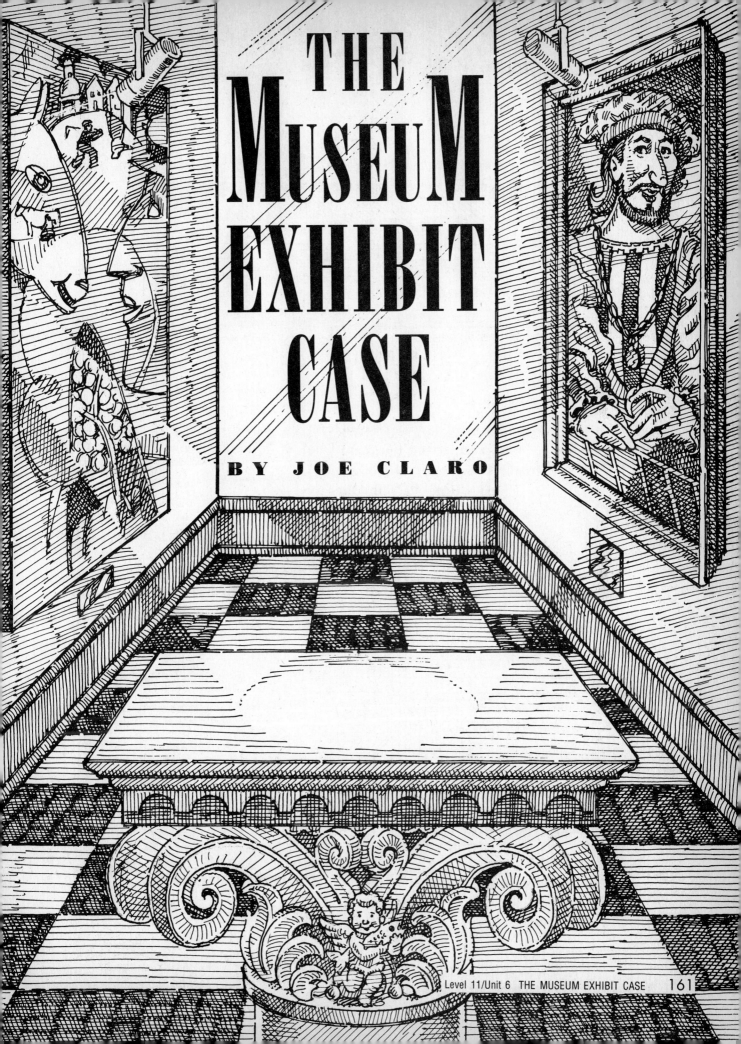

THE MUSEUM EXHIBIT CASE

BY JOE CLARO

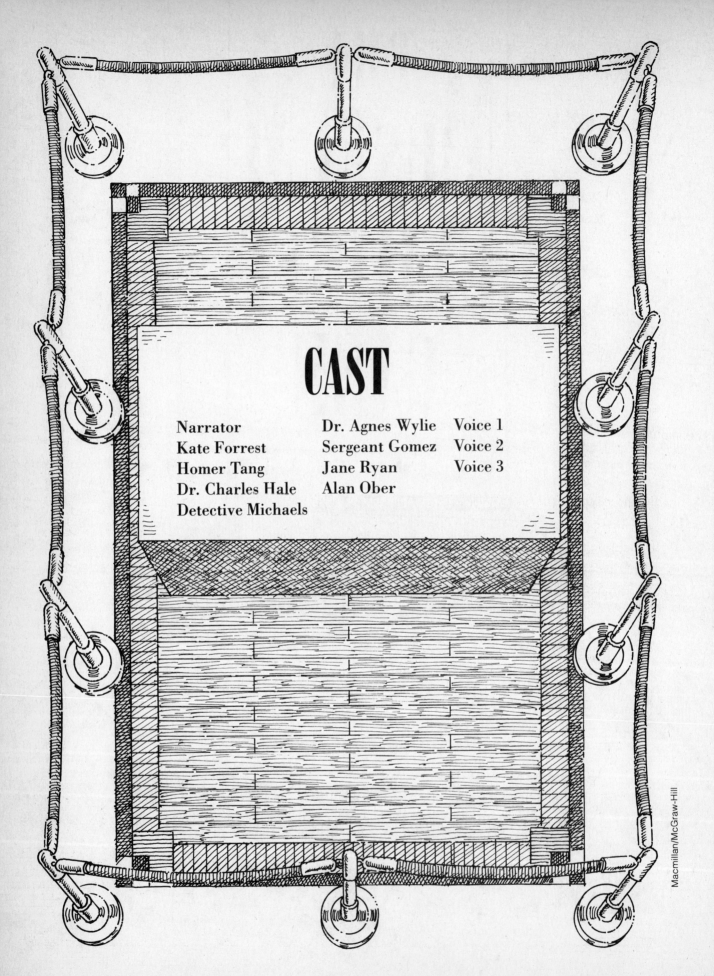

CAST

Narrator
Kate Forrest
Homer Tang
Dr. Charles Hale
Detective Michaels

Dr. Agnes Wylie
Sergeant Gomez
Jane Ryan
Alan Ober

Voice 1
Voice 2
Voice 3

NARRATOR: The Museum of Art was like a second home to Kate Forrest and Homer Tang. Ever since kindergarten, they had visited the exhibits and attended special classes there. But because it was such a large museum, there was still lots to explore, so they had signed up for a class called Discover the Museum. This class, given during spring vacation, would give them a chance to investigate all the parts of the building—the public areas as well as the private ones behind the scenes.

KATE: Hi, Homer. Were you able to finish your project for today's class?

HOMER: Morning, Kate. Yeah, I was able to get it done, but it took me a lot more time than I thought it would. Drawing a floor plan of the ground floor of this museum isn't that easy!

KATE: I know. I thought I knew this museum inside and out, but it's hard to remember where all the exhibits are—even after spending so much time here. We still have a few minutes before class starts. Do you want to check your drawing with the scale model in the lobby?

HOMER: That's a good . . . hey, Kate, look at that! There are police in the African wing.

KATE: They've roped off one of the exhibits. I wonder what happened.

NARRATOR: Kate and Homer hurried over to the area in front of a large glass case, where a curious crowd had begun to gather. Observing the police at work was Charles Hale, the assistant director of the museum.

KATE: Hello, Dr. Hale. What's going on?

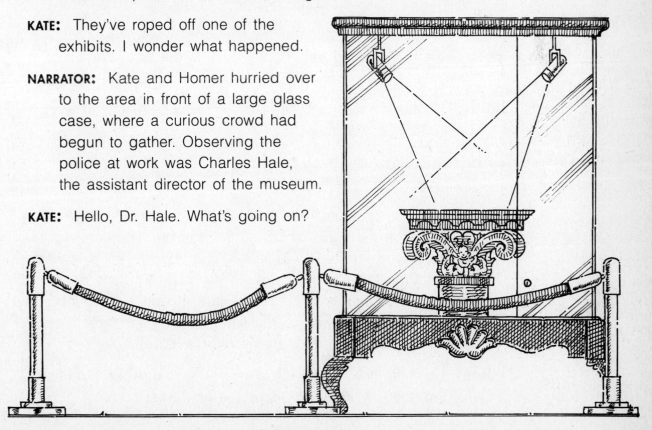

DR. HALE: Hi, Kate and Homer. There was a robbery here last night. It looks as if someone managed to open one of the exhibit cases. Several artifacts are missing.

HOMER: What kind of artifacts?

DR. HALE: They were small items, but all quite valuable—beautiful gold ornaments from the kingdom of Benin.

KATE: I don't understand how a thief could get in here. Isn't the museum checked after it closes at night?

HOMER: And aren't all the cases connected to some kind of alarm-system?

DR. HALE: Yes, to both those questions. And there's a third point that's puzzling the police; they aren't sure how the thief got *out* of the museum. All the doors were still locked this morning, and none of the alarms were triggered. It's possible that . . . on second thought, I'd probably better not say anything more—confidential security information, you know.

HOMER: Wow! This sounds like a real mystery.

DR. HALE: You're right about that! Well, it looks as if the police are finished here, so I'd better get back to my office. See you two later.

KATE: So long, Dr. Hale. Hey, Homer, look at the time. We're late for class. They've probably left for the exhibit area already.

HOMER: It's okay. If we go straight to the Colonial American wing, we'll catch up with them.

KATE: Right. Let's just check the model to make sure we know the quickest way to get there.

NARRATOR: Kate and Homer cut through the main lobby for a quick look at the scale model of the museum. People used it all the time to find their way around the huge building. It was an exact miniature of the museum, complete with tiny paintings and artifacts, small figures of visitors, and a museum guard in uniform. It was so realistic that the little clock in the great hall even had hands that could be moved.

HOMER: Let's see now. . . . The Colonial American wing is on the second floor, right? Here it is, in the northwest corner.

KATE: If we walk down the main corridor, then go upstairs and turn right, we should be there in no time. Let's hurry. I don't want to miss any of the colonial craft demonstrations.

HOMER: I'm right behind you!

NARRATOR: The police were also moving on. After finishing his inspection of the scene of the robbery, Chief Detective Michaels and his assistant, Sergeant Gomez, headed for the administrative offices. There they found Dr. Agnes Wylie, the museum director.

DET. MICHAELS: I think we've done all we can for today, Dr. Wylie. I'm sorry to say that fingerprints are of absolutely no use in this case.

DR. WYLIE: You mean there are none?

DET. MICHAELS: No, just the opposite—there are too many! The museum cases are covered with them. It's impossible to sort them all out.

DR. WYLIE: Have you been able to figure out how the thief got in and out of the building?

DET. MICHAELS: No, we haven't. We've checked every entrance and exit, but there's no sign of illegal or forced entry.

SGT. GOMEZ: Something that might help us is a list of employees who had access to the African wing last night.

DR. WYLIE: Surely you don't suspect one of our own employees? Do you have any idea of what a thorough background check the museum does before we hire someone?

DET. MICHAELS: I believe we do, Dr. Wylie. Still, if you don't mind, we'd like that list. Until we have something definite to go on, no one is beyond suspicion.

SGT. GOMEZ: By the way, have there been any other robberies in the museum recently?

DR. WYLIE: Not that we know of. However, I'm planning to have each department curator do a complete inventory. My assistant, Dr. Hale, will be in charge. Mr. Ober will help him. I assume you've already met Mr. Ober, the head of museum security. Anyway, if anything else is missing, of course I'll let you know immediately.

DET. MICHAELS: Thank you, Dr. Wylie. We'll be in touch.

NARRATOR: That afternoon, Dr. Wylie met with Dr. Hale and Mr. Ober in the conference room. When they were through discussing the plans for the inventory, the three of them headed back to her office, still trying to unravel the mystery of the theft.

SOUND EFFECT: [*phone ringing*]

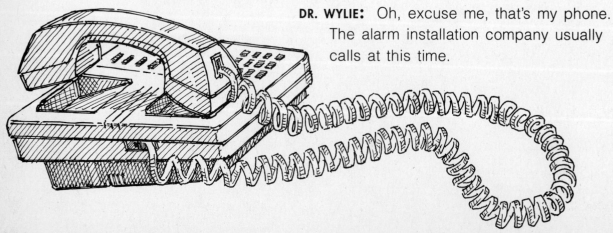

DR. WYLIE: Oh, excuse me, that's my phone. The alarm installation company usually calls at this time.

Macmillan/McGraw-Hill

NARRATOR: As she rushed into her office to pick up her phone, Dr. Wylie almost tripped over a vacuum cleaner that was propped up against her desk. The cleaning woman, Jane Ryan, immediately moved the vacuum out of the way.

JANE RYAN: Sorry, Dr. Wylie. I thought you were gone for the day. I wouldn't have left it there otherwise.

DR. WYLIE: No harm done. I just have to get to that phone. Hello? . . . Yes, this is Dr. Wylie. . . . Just a minute, let me write that down. Alarm off tonight. . . . What time? . . . I see. How many more nights will you need to complete the installation of the new alarm-system? . . . Only three more? Well, that's a relief! Thank you, I'll speak to you tomorrow.

NARRATOR: Dr. Wylie tore her scribbled note off the pad and left her office. Minutes later, a gloved hand reached for the pad and tore off the next sheet of paper. At about the same time, Kate and Homer were on their way out of the museum.

HOMER: That class was great. I really liked dipping candles. We can use them for the holidays.

KATE: Yeah, they look nice. How do you like my tin lantern?

HOMER: It looks just like an original Paul Revere.

KATE: Thanks. Where do we go tomorrow?

HOMER: The Egyptian wing. Maybe they'll let us unwrap a mummy!

KATE: Oh, sure! Let's stop in the lobby and check the model on our way out. That way we can find the place we're supposed to meet tomorrow.

HOMER: Okay. Let's see . . . the Egyptian wing . . . First Dynasty Room . . . here it is, down the hall from the Greek vases.

KATE: Hey, that's funny.

HOMER: What is?

KATE: Look at the security guard in the model. Wasn't it in the African wing when we came in today?

HOMER: I think so. And now it's in the Native American wing. How do you suppose it got moved? Here comes Dr. Hale. Let's ask him about it.

DR. HALE: Hi, Kate. Hi, Homer. Are you leaving now?

KATE: Yes, but we'd like to ask you something before we go. Look at this figure of the guard in the museum model.

DR. HALE: Yes, I've seen it. Amazing how accurate the detail is, considering the fact that it's only three inches high.

HOMER: No, Kate means look at *where* it is.

DR. HALE: Uh-huh, it's right there in the Native American wing. What about it?

KATE: This morning it was in the African wing.

DR. HALE: So?

KATE: Well, why is it in another spot now?

DR. HALE: Who knows? I guess whoever dusted the model inadvertently moved it to a different place.

HOMER: Oh, I see. I didn't realize it had to be dusted.

KATE: Sure, that makes sense. That's probably how the hands of the clock got moved, too. They were at 11:00 when we were here this morning, and now they're set at 12:00.

SOUND EFFECT: [*clanging bell*]

HOMER: There's the closing bell. We'd better get going. Bye, Dr. Hale.

DR. HALE: So long.

NARRATOR: The heavy doors of the museum swung shut for the day. The sun set, and soon the building was dark, except for the few lights left on for the security people. At precisely one minute after midnight, a figure slipped out of a closet on the second floor, and moved silently and surely down the shadowy halls to the Native American wing. A hand unlocked exhibit case 43, reached in, and took the only object on display—a beautifully carved and painted wooden doll with a feathered headdress. Then, just as silently, the figure swiftly returned to the closet and closed the door. The following morning, shortly after the museum opened, the theft was discovered.

MR. OBER: Agnes, the new Hopi Kachina doll is gone! Case 43 is empty.

DR. WYLIE: When will this end? I'll call Detective Michaels right away.

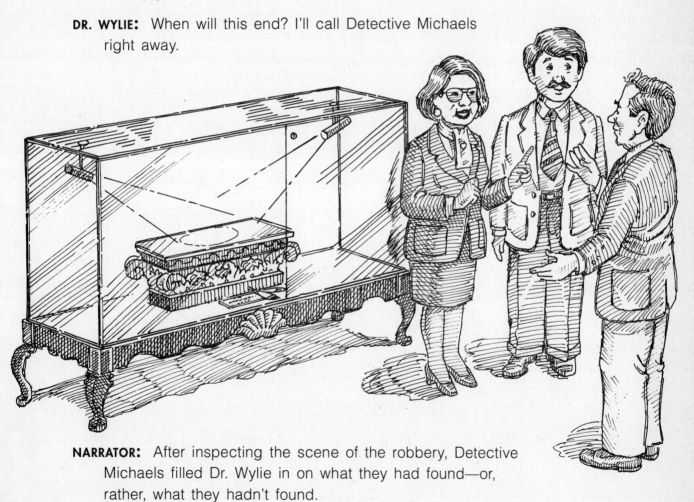

NARRATOR: After inspecting the scene of the robbery, Detective Michaels filled Dr. Wylie in on what they had found—or, rather, what they hadn't found.

DET. MICHAELS: When a crime is this clean, it usually means one thing. It's an inside job.

DR. WYLIE: An inside job? You still think that someone who works at the museum is committing these robberies? But, as I told you yesterday, all our applicants are thoroughly screened before we hire them.

DET. MICHAELS: I know, Dr. Wylie. But we have to check out every possibility, including this one. Now, let's begin with the people who have access to all parts of the museum after hours.

DR. WYLIE: Well, of course I have access to the whole building, and so does Alan Ober, our head of security.

SGT. GOMEZ: Anyone else?

DR. WYLIE: Just one other person . . . uh, Charles Hale, my assistant.

DET. MICHAELS: Why did you hesitate before mentioning him?

DR. WYLIE: Well, I have mixed feelings about Charles. On the one hand, he's very good at his job.

DET. MICHAELS: And on the other hand?

DR. WYLIE: I think he'd give anything to have *my* job.

DET. MICHAELS: Does "anything" include stealing from the museum to make you look bad?

DR. WYLIE: Goodness, no! I really don't think Charles would go that far. Listen, Detective Michaels, I'm not trying to cast suspicion on anyone.

DET. MICHAELS: You don't have to. I'm suspicious by nature! Now, how many new employees have you hired in the past, let's say, six months?

DR. WYLIE: Not many. You see, we don't have that many openings. This is a nice place to work, and people don't quit very often. In the last six months, we've only hired two new people.

SGT. GOMEZ: And who are they?

DR. WYLIE: There's Amanda Green, in our gift store. She's the granddaughter of one of our museum trustees. And there's a new cleaning woman, Jane Ryan, who started about two months ago. There isn't anything in either of their backgrounds that would arouse suspicion.

DET. MICHAELS: All right, one last question. Have any employees left here in the last year with, shall we say, hard feelings?

DR. WYLIE: Oh, no. People who leave us are usually retiring or moving on to other jobs.

SGT. GOMEZ: Isn't anyone ever fired?

DR. WYLIE: Well, now that you mention it, there was a security guard who was fired about a year ago. What was his name? Let me think. . . . Oh, yes, I remember now. It was a man by the name of Donegan. Mr. Ober found him sleeping on the job—more than once. Eventually, he had to fire the man. I remember it because Donegan was very upset and angry. It was an unpleasant situation.

DET. MICHAELS: Thanks, Dr. Wylie. Maybe what you've told us will lead somewhere.

DR. WYLIE: I doubt it, Detective Michaels. Mr. Donegan wasn't the kind of man who would break into a locked building. And as for the new employees, I trust our personnel department to hire only the most reliable people.

DET. MICHAELS: All the same, we'll do a bit of checking down at police headquarters.

SGT. GOMEZ: Besides, as of now, we have nothing else to go on.

NARRATOR: A few days later, Dr. Wylie asked Alan Ober and Charles Hale to meet with her in her office.

DR. WYLIE: Charles, have the curators finished their inventories yet?

DR. HALE: Yes, I just got the last report. You're not going to like what they've found.

DR. WYLIE: What is it?

MR. OBER: We haven't been robbed twice, as we all thought. We've found evidence of three other robberies since our last museum-wide inventory!

DR. WYLIE: Five thefts all together? I can't believe it! Furthermore, I don't understand how these robberies could have gone unnoticed.

DR. HALE: The earlier thefts involved small items whose absence from the exhibit cases could have been easily overlooked. The inventory revealed things missing from the musical instrument collection, the Greek wing, and the prehistoric exhibit, in addition to what was taken this week.

DR. WYLIE: This is dreadful! We certainly aren't dealing with any ordinary burglar. These robberies appear to have been cleverly planned and carried out.

MR. OBER: That's right. We've discovered something else, too. Our last major inventory was completed the day before the installation of the new alarm-system began.

DR. WYLIE: I see. That means all the robberies have taken place within the last two weeks, and . . .

DR. HALE: . . . and the thief had to know that a new alarm was being installed—a fact that we've kept top secret.

MR. OBER: I'd say that points to this being an inside job, Agnes.

DR. WYLIE: That's exactly what Detective Michaels said.

MR. OBER: He did? Does he know something you haven't told me about?

DR. WYLIE: Why no, Alan. Why would you think that?

Macmillan/McGraw-Hill

MR. OBER: It sounds like there are things being kept from me. I *am* the head of security here, and I should be aware of everything that's been learned in this investigation.

DR. WYLIE: Alan, nothing has been learned—that's precisely the problem! As soon as the police discover anything, you'll know about it immediately, rest assured.

NARRATOR: At that moment, Jane Ryan, pushing her cart laden with cleaning supplies, opened the door to Dr. Wylie's office.

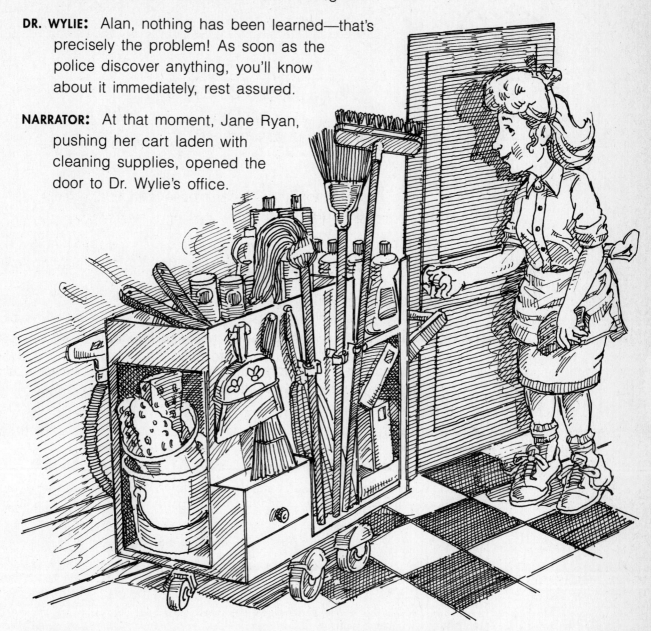

JANE RYAN: Oh, excuse me, Dr. Wylie. I didn't know you were still here.

DR. WYLIE: I didn't realize it was so late! We won't be much longer, Jane.

JANE RYAN: That's all right; there's no hurry. I'll start by cleaning Dr. Hale's office first.

DR. HALE: Come on, Jane. I'll walk down the hall and unlock my door for you. I need to pick up a few things before I go home.

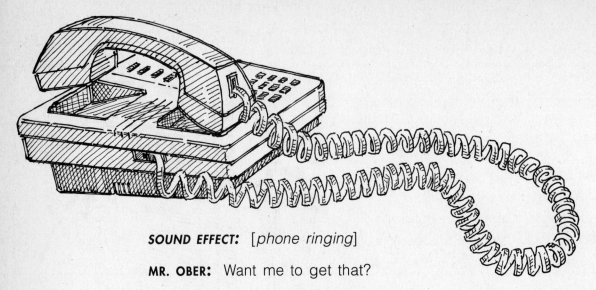

SOUND EFFECT: [*phone ringing*]

MR. OBER: Want me to get that?

DR. WYLIE: That's all right, Alan, I've got it. Hello? . . . Yes, this is Dr. Wylie. . . . You'll be working on the alarm tonight starting at 11:30? Where? . . . Let me jot that down. All right, I've got it. Thank you.

NARRATOR: Dr. Wylie tore the sheet of paper off her notepad.

DR. WYLIE: Alan, here's the information about the new alarm-system. They'll be doing the Asian wing tonight. Only two more nights of this and the new system will be in, thank goodness.

MR. OBER: Yes, it'll be a relief to have this over with. I've never liked having the alarm turned off at night, even if it is in only one wing at a time. Let's take a walk down there now and just make sure that all the exhibit cases are securely locked.

NARRATOR: As the two left the office, they passed Dr. Hale in the corridor.

DR. HALE: I think I left my portfolio in Dr. Wylie's office.

MR. OBER: I didn't notice it.

DR. HALE: I'd better go back and make sure.

NARRATOR: A short time later, a gloved hand reached for the notepad on the desk. The sound of a sheet of paper being torn off was followed by soft footsteps and the click of the closing door. About an hour later, Kate and Homer were walking through the main hall.

KATE: Let's stop at the model for a second. I want to check on something for our next assignment.

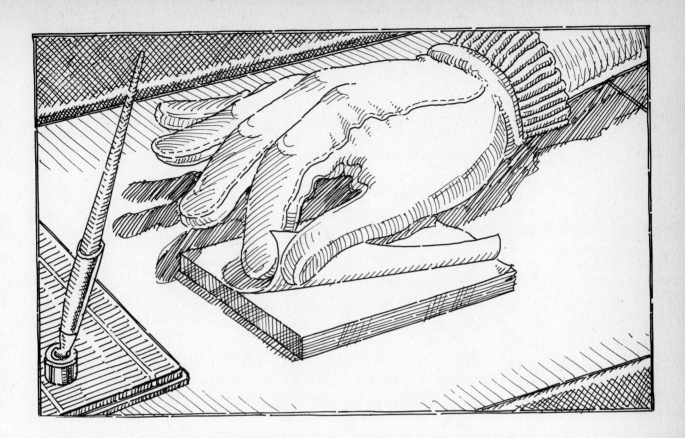

HOMER: Okay, and we can see what area we'll be in tomorrow, too. We're scheduled to go behind the scenes in the Roman wing. I think it's on the lower level.

KATE: That'll be great. I'll bet we're going to see how . . . Homer! Look at the figure of the security guard!

HOMER: It's in the Asian wing. So what?

KATE: It wasn't there this morning. It was over here, in the Native American wing.

HOMER: So, it's been moved again. Somebody probably dusted.

KATE: The hands of the clock are set at a different time, too. Don't you think it's kind of weird?

HOMER: Well, maybe. Come to think of it, none of the other figures seem to be in different places.

KATE: Here comes Dr. Wylie. Let's see what she thinks.

HOMER: Dr. Wylie, do you know anything about this scale model?

DR. WYLIE: Well, it was donated to the museum by Henry Pierpont Vandergilt in 1933. Over the years, we've added to it to reflect the new wings that have opened.

KATE: Uh . . . a history of the model was not exactly what we had in mind, Dr. Wylie.

HOMER: You see, we've noticed something funny. Dr. Hale didn't think it was important, but we thought we'd ask you.

DR. WYLIE: What have you noticed?

HOMER: The security-guard figure . . . it keeps showing up in different parts of the museum.

KATE: You see, yesterday morning it was in the African wing, but by closing time, it was in the Native American wing. This morning, it was still in the Native American wing, but now it's in the Asian wing. It always seems to get moved late in the afternoon.

DR. WYLIE: My guess is that the model is probably dusted about the same time every day, and whoever dusts moves the guard figure. We've never told anyone not to, because it doesn't really matter.

HOMER: Dr. Hale said just about the same thing.

KATE: The hands on the clock get changed, too. This morning they were set at 12:00. Now, they're at 11:30.

DR. WYLIE: Sounds like somebody's playing. . . . Wait a minute! Did you say the guard was in the African wing and then in the Native American wing?

KATE: Yes.

DR. WYLIE: Can you remember what day that was?

HOMER: Sure, it was yesterday.

DR. WYLIE: And now the figure is in the Asian wing. That's very interesting.

KATE: Do you really think so?

DR. WYLIE: Yes, I do. Thanks. I'll see you both later.

NARRATOR: Dr. Wylie hurried back to her office to call Detective Michaels and ask him to come to the museum. She indicated that she had something important to discuss with him, and explained that she didn't want to do it over the telephone. When he arrived, Dr. Wylie summarized what Kate and Homer had told her.

DET. MICHAELS: All right, so the security-guard figure has been moved a few times. Certainly that could happen when the model was dusted.

DR. WYLIE: But don't you see? Yesterday, the guard was moved from the African wing to the Native American wing. And those are the two wings in which the robberies took place.

SGT. GOMEZ: Dr. Wylie, that could be coincidence.

DR. WYLIE: You think so? Well, what about this? Tonight the new alarm system is being installed in the Asian wing.

DET. MICHAELS: Yes?

DR. WYLIE: That's where the figure of the guard has now been placed—in the Asian wing. I think there's a good chance that we're going to be robbed again.

DET. MICHAELS: That may be. But, Dr. Wylie, I don't see how moving that little toy security guard around is helping someone break into the museum and get out again—all without opening any doors or setting off any alarms.

DR. WYLIE: Well, maybe the thief knows that the alarms are going be turned off in those areas.

SGT. GOMEZ: But how would the thief know what time the alarm system was going to be turned off? Didn't you tell us that it is purposely turned off at different times every night?

DR. WYLIE: Yes, that's why I think you're right about it being an inside job. You can't deny that those children have noticed something that looks like a pretty funny coincidence.

DET. MICHAELS: You may be on to something, Dr. Wylie. Didn't you mention that the kids told you something about the clock in the model? What exactly did they say?

NARRATOR: Dr. Wylie repeated what Kate and Homer had observed, and Detective Michaels suddenly looked interested.

DET. MICHAELS: That information makes the whole thing seem like more than just a coincidence. Let's back up just a minute, Dr. Wylie. Describe for me once more what happens when you get the phone call from the alarm installation company.

NARRATOR: Dr. Wylie explained exactly what she did from the time she got the phone call.

DET. MICHAELS: Yeah, I'm beginning to see a pattern here. We'll check out the museum model immediately.

DR. WYLIE: How will you do that?

DET. MICHAELS: First, we'll move the figure of the guard to another area in the model, and change the hands on the clock. You would probably be the best person to do that. Then I'll place one of my people in a position to watch what happens.

DR. WYLIE: And then can you make an arrest and put an end to this trouble?

DET. MICHAELS: I'm afraid it's not quite so simple, Dr. Wylie. Moving the guard and the hands of the clock in the scale model isn't exactly a crime. But if we spot someone doing it, we may have a way of catching the thief tonight.

NARRATOR: Detective Michaels made a phone call, and in a short time a plainclothes police officer took her position on the balcony of the museum. From there, she had a clear view of the scale model. At closing time, she reported to Detective Michaels, who then met with Dr. Wylie in her office.

DR. WYLIE: Did your police officer find out anything, Detective Michaels?

DET. MICHAELS: Maybe. We can't be sure. Alan Ober spent some time standing around the scale model. But he didn't touch anything. Later on, those two kids showed up.

DR. WYLIE: You mean Homer and Kate.

DET. MICHAELS: Yes. While they were studying the model, your assistant came by.

DR. WYLIE: And did Charles move anything?

DET. MICHAELS: He did. While he was talking to Kate and Homer, he picked up the guard figure and put it down in the Asian wing. But that certainly isn't conclusive evidence.

SGT. GOMEZ: When he left, we had to do some fast work and move it out of the Asian wing again. But we spotted Mr. Ober coming back, so we had to get out of there. There wasn't time to check the clock.

DR. WYLIE: Did Alan stop at the model again?

SGT. GOMEZ: Yes, he did. He took a few minutes to talk to a visitor, pointed to the model, and then he moved on.

DR. WYLIE: Oh, my. This is getting confusing. What happened next?

DET. MICHAELS: At precisely 4:30, one of the people on your cleaning staff came to dust—it was Jane Ryan. When she was finished, the figure had been moved again.

DR. WYLIE: Where did she put it?

DET. MICHAELS: In the Asian wing.

DR. WYLIE: Jane Ryan? I can't believe she could have anything to do with this. How could she possibly know anything about where or when the alarm would be turned off? What about the clock? Was it changed?

SGT. GOMEZ: Yes, it was. I hate to say this, but people passing by the model repeatedly blocked our plainclothes officer's view. So we don't know who moved the hands on the clock.

DR. WYLIE: Well, I think you can eliminate Jane Ryan as a suspect. She doesn't have a motive, and, besides, she doesn't know anything about our procedures.

DET. MICHAELS: You know, Dr. Wylie, if there's one thing I've learned in my years on the force, it's that things aren't always what they seem to be.

DR. WYLIE: So what will you do now?

DET. MICHAELS: I'm going to arrange a little trap!

Macmillan/McGraw-Hill

NARRATOR: That night, there were several figures in the Asian wing who were definitely not a part of the exhibits. They watched as someone crept up to one of the cases, unlocked it, and removed a priceless lacquered fan studded with emeralds and rubies.

VOICE 1: [*Off-Stage Voices*] Police officers! Hold it right there.

VOICE 2: We'll take that, if you don't mind.

VOICE 3: What? Police? Let go of me!

VOICE 1: Come along, please. There are a few questions we'd like to ask you as soon as we inform you of your rights!

VOICE 3: All right. I guess you caught me red-handed. I'll tell you anything you want to know.

NARRATOR: The following afternoon, Jane Ryan arrived at work at her usual time. She punched her time-card, hung up her coat, and went to the closet where her cleaning supplies were kept. She reached in the closet and took a large brown paper bag down off one of the shelves.

DET. MICHAELS: Hold it right there, ma'am! I'll take that bag!

JANE RYAN: Oh! You startled me! Who are you? What are you doing hiding behind that pillar?

DET. MICHAELS: I'm Detective Michaels of the Metropolitan Police Department. And I think you know why I'm here.

JANE RYAN: I don't know what you're talking about. *I'm* here to get my cleaning supplies.

DET. MICHAELS: No, you aren't, Mrs. Ryan. You came to pick up this paper bag that you then planned to take down to the locker room.

JANE RYAN: You must be mistaken. I don't even know what's inside that bag.

DET. MICHAELS: I think you do. You know that this bag contains some items taken from the Asian wing last night. You know that your father took them while the alarm was turned off. And you know that there are several similar bags in your locker. What you may not know is that we apprehended your father in the Asian wing late last night and arrested him. He's told us everything.

NARRATOR: After Jane Ryan was taken down to the station for questioning, Detective Michaels met with Dr. Wylie, Charles Hale, and Alan Ober.

DR. WYLIE: So the guard and the clock in the model were part of a signaling system after all!

DET. MICHAELS: Yes. Jane Ryan's father would check the scale model just before the museum closed to find out where the guard figure was placed and to see the time on the clock. Then he'd hide himself in her cleaning closet until the alarm was disconnected.

SGT. GOMEZ: When he knew the alarm was off, he'd open one of the display cases with a skeleton key he'd copied from her key ring. Then he'd take the items he'd decided on, and go back to the closet to hide. He'd hide the stolen artifacts in an ordinary paper bag, and leave them in the closet for his daughter to pick up when she came in to work the next day.

DET. MICHAELS: The next morning, he'd slip out of the closet when the museum had filled up. Then he'd stroll toward the exit and leave the building just like any other visitor.

MR. OBER: But how did Jane Ryan know we were installing a new alarm system? That information was known only to Dr. Wylie, Dr. Hale, and me.

DET. MICHAELS: Apparently, she was cleaning Dr. Wylie's office on the day when the first phone call came in about the alarm system. She overheard the conversation and told her father about it. Then he got the idea of how to use that information to his advantage.

DR. WYLIE: So she knew that a new alarm system was being put in, but I still don't understand how she knew when and where the alarm would be turned off.

DET. MICHAELS: Well, *you* actually gave us the answer to that piece of the puzzle, Dr. Wylie. You told us that whenever you received the phone call from the installation company, you always wrote down the information on a notepad.

SGT. GOMEZ: Jane Ryan knew that you always got that call in the afternoon, so she made sure to clean your office late in the day. Once she was in your office, it was simple to get the information from your notepad.

DR. WYLIE: But how? I always tore off the sheet of paper I wrote on and took it to the security office.

FROM THE DESK OF...
AGNES WYLIE

Alarm
Asian Wing
11:30 P.M.

DET. MICHAELS: Right. But the impression of your writing went through to the *next* sheet of paper on the pad. All Mrs. Ryan had to do was to tear that sheet off and use the edge of a pencil to shade the paper. That made the writing show up.

SGT. GOMEZ: She passed the information on to her father by means of the scale model of the museum. She'd put the guard in the wing where the new alarm would be installed, and set the hands of the clock to the hour that indicated when the old alarm would be turned off.

DR. HALE: That was pretty ingenious. But why did they keep all the stolen items in paper bags in her locker? They were small enough to be carried out of the building without anyone knowing about it.

DET. MICHAELS: Ah, well, now we come to the motive. It was never their intention to sell the items they had stolen.

MR. OBER: Huh? That doesn't make sense. What was their intention if they didn't plan to sell them?

DET. MICHAELS: To frame *you*!

MR. OBER: What!

DET. MICHAELS: Jane Ryan was going to plant the stolen goods in your locker or in your office—someplace that she had access to. Then she was going to make an anonymous phone call to the police and accuse you of theft.

DR. WYLIE: But why would they want to frame Alan?

DET. MICHAELS: Oh, didn't I mention that her name before she was married was Jane *Donegan*?

MR. OBER: You mean her father is Michael Donegan, the man I had to fire about a year ago? I can't believe it!

SGT. GOMEZ: Yup, he's the one. His daughter took the job here at the museum hoping to find a way that she and her father could get even with you. Donegan grew a beard and a mustache so that he could go around the museum without being recognized.

Macmillan/McGraw-Hill

DR. WYLIE: Well, you detectives have done a fine job! I can't begin to tell you how grateful we all are.

DET. MICHAELS: Thank you, Dr. Wylie. But I have two people outside who deserve a good part of the credit.

DR. WYLIE: Who're they?

DET. MICHAELS: Why, Kate and Homer. They gave us our first real clue to solving this mystery.

DR. WYLIE: That's true. I wish there were some way of rewarding them.

DR. HALE: They both love this museum—they practically live here! Maybe we could give them an honorary membership for a year. Then they could take all the classes they wanted to free of charge. When the new Arms and Armor exhibit opens, they'll probably want to move in.

DR. WYLIE: That's a wonderful idea, Charles. Say . . . speaking of the new Arms and Armor exhibit, how about asking them to cut the ribbon at the opening ceremony?

DR. HALE: Great! Let's call them in and tell them.

NARRATOR: Kate and Homer couldn't believe their ears.

HOMER: You want us to cut the ribbon?

KATE: A year's membership—free?

HOMER/KATE: That's great!

NARRATOR: For an added treat, Dr. Wylie let Homer and Kate stay in the museum after hours that day. They went along as Dr. Wylie and Detective Michaels made sure that all the stolen items were returned to their proper cases. Both the museum director and the chief of detectives gave a big sigh of relief as the last case was locked.

DR. WYLIE: Well, that does it.

DET. MICHAELS: This case is closed!

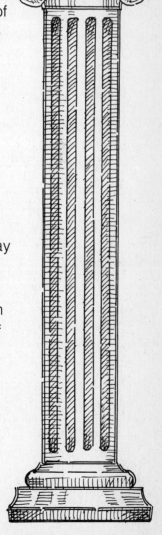

BLOCKING DIAGRAM

Arrange eleven stools and a screen, as shown. The narrator can use a music stand to hold the script.

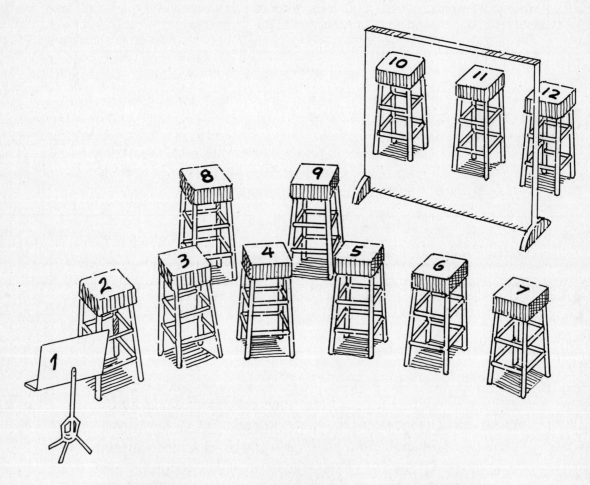

1. NARRATOR	5. DR. AGNES WYLIE	9. SGT. GOMEZ
2. KATE FORREST	6. ALAN OBER	10. VOICE 1
3. HOMER TANG	7. JANE RYAN	11. VOICE 2
4. DR. CHARLES HALE	8. DET. MICHAELS	12. VOICE 3

Macmillan/McGraw-Hill

Readers Theater Plays

After appearing in a Readers Theater production or two, students are often sparked to write a Readers Theater script of their own. The following student resource pages are designed to help guide your students through the process.

Creating a Readers Theater script not only develops writing skills, but also extends students' understanding of story elements. Students must closely examine plot, setting, characterization, and motivation to transform a narrative into a drama. One of the challenges students face in writing a Readers Theater script is how to convey action and changes in time and place without using the stage directions available to the author of a conventional play. If students adapt a story, they must make choices about what to include and what to omit. If they write an original play, they are faced with other decisions: how to invent a story line that builds dramatic tension, and how to make the characters believable. If students choose to write a play based on historical events, they will need to determine what research is necessary to ensure historical accuracy.

Before students begin writing their own Readers Theater plays, it may be helpful to explore with them the differences between narrative and drama. One way to do this is to obtain a copy of the folk tale "The Case of the Uncooked Eggs" collected by Diane Wolkstein (see the Bibliography on page xii). First, read an episode from the story; then read the same episode in the Readers Theater script in this book. Help students compare the two so that they begin to understand the differences in structure and in the methods used to communicate information, action, and characterization. Discuss how the narrative is transformed into dialog. Guide students to see that in Readers Theater, a narrator provides transitions from one setting or time to another, and describes action that cannot be conveyed through dialog. Point out that the three neighbors function as narrators in the Readers Theater version of "The Case of the Uncooked Eggs." Then have students examine the narrators' roles. Finally, have students identify portions of the story that differ in the play, and scenes from the play that do not appear in the story at all. Encourage students to speculate on reasons for these changes.

After students grasp some of the major differences between stories and plays, introduce the following writing-process worksheets to guide them through the steps of creating their own Readers Theater plays. When writing a script, students can work individually, in small cooperative-writing groups, or as an entire class.

If your students choose to adapt a folk tale or legend, suggest that they read several versions of the story before they begin to write. If students decide to adapt a story or a book, a reading followed by group discussion will ensure that all students are familiar with the plot, characters, and setting. If students choose to write an original play, they will need to create the plot, characters, and setting themselves.

GETTING STARTED

Take a minute to think about the Readers Theater plays in which you have participated. Did you ever say to yourself, "I think I can write a play like this"? If you did, you were right! Writing a Readers Theater play isn't that difficult once you know how.

GETTING AN IDEA FOR A PLAY

The first question you will need to answer when writing a play is, "What should my play be about?" The answer can be found in two familiar places—your *experience* and your *imagination*. You may not realize it, but you've probably had dozens of experiences that you can call upon for ideas.

Here are some possible sources:

- personal experiences you've had at home, at school, or on a trip
- stories you've read in books or magazines
- programs you've seen on TV or movies that you've watched
- real-life events you've read about in social studies books, or in newspapers or magazines

Macmillan/McGraw-Hill

Remember, when writing about personal experiences or something you've read, you don't have to be limited by what actually happened. By using your imagination, you can turn the experience or the reading into your own original creation. Your imagination is important even when writing a play about a historical event. While the characters and events may be based on fact, your imagination will help you create conversations between the characters.

Get together with a partner or a small group of classmates. Brainstorm at least one idea for each of the sources listed on page 188. Use another sheet of paper to record your ideas. Here's an example of a play idea based on a folk tale that may help you get started.

I read a Japanese folk tale called "The Stonecutter." It is about a man who becomes unhappy with his life as a stonecutter. One day, he wishes to be rich and powerful. His wish is granted, and he is happy for a short time. However, he soon wishes to be someone even richer or more powerful. Each time this happens, his wish is granted, but the stonecutter is never satisfied. It is only when he becomes a stonecutter once again that he realizes he was happiest as a simple stonecutter.

THE PLOT

WHAT IS A PLOT? WHY IS IT IMPORTANT?

When you describe what happens in a play, you are talking about the plot of the play. A plot is a series of events that tell a story. A plot has a beginning, a middle, and an end. Most plays begin with a problem. The middle of the play deals with the characters' attempts to solve the problem. The end of the play reveals how the problem is finally solved.

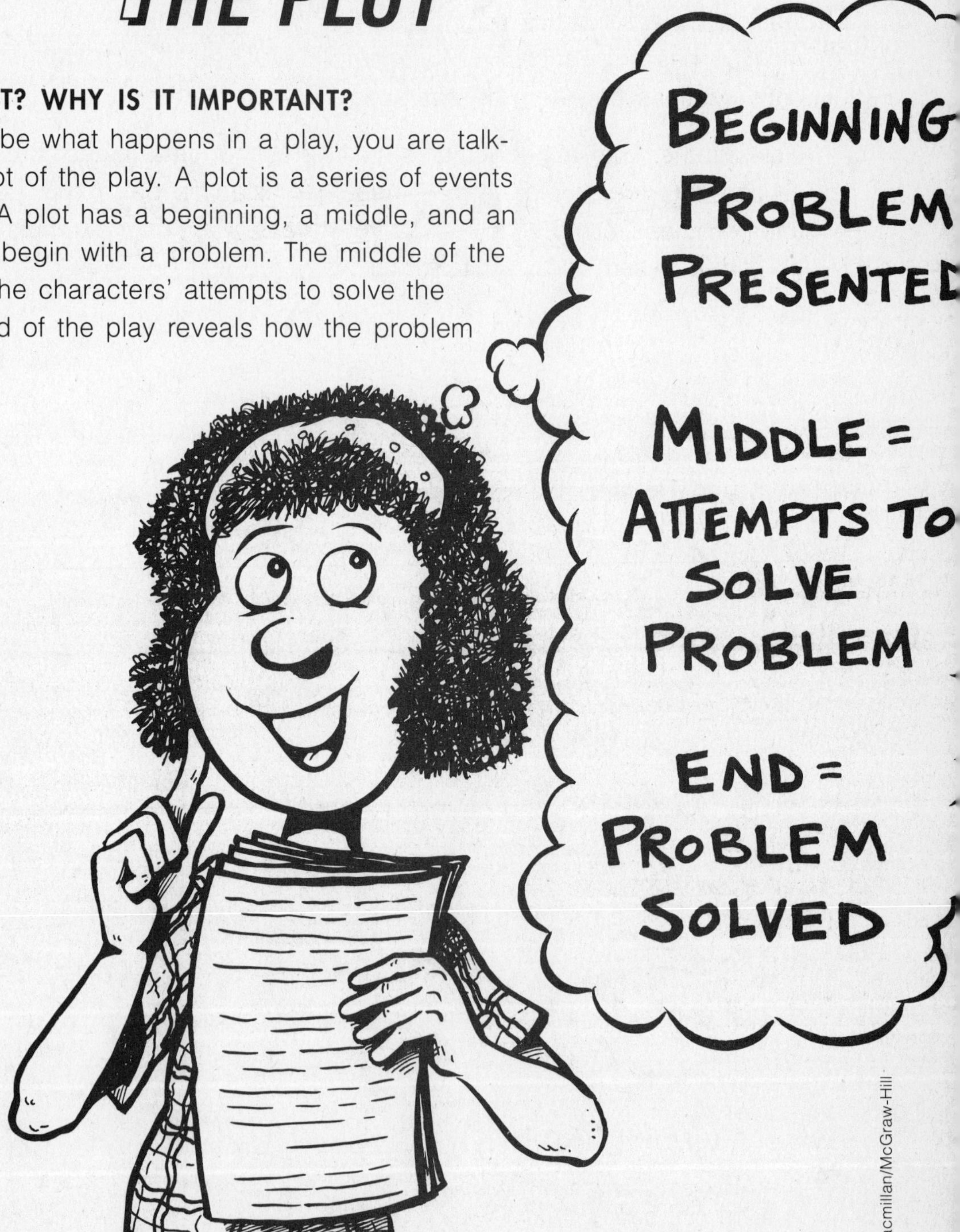

BEGINNING
PROBLEM
PRESENTED

MIDDLE =
ATTEMPTS TO
SOLVE
PROBLEM

END =
PROBLEM
SOLVED

Macmillan/McGraw-Hill

Here is a simple plot outline for the folk tale described on the "Getting Started" page.

Beginning: A stonecutter cuts stone from a huge mountain. A spirit who can grant wishes lives in the mountain but the stonecutter has never seen or heard this spirit. One day when delivering stone to a rich man, the stonecutter sees many beautiful things in the house. He wishes that he were rich, and a voice tells him that his wish is granted.

Middle: When the stonecutter returns home, he finds a beautiful house instead of his hut. He is happy until he sees a prince, and then the stonecutter wishes to be a prince. Again his wish is granted, but he is still not satisfied. He sees that the sun is more powerful than a prince, so he asks to become the sun. When he discovers that a rain cloud can cover the sun, he wishes to be a rain cloud. When he finds that rain has no effect on a rock, he wishes to be a rock. He is happy until a stonecutter comes by. As the stonecutter begins to cut, he understands that a man is more powerful than a rock, and he wishes to be a man.

End: This wish, like the others, is granted, and he becomes a stonecutter once more. At last he is happy, and never again does he long to be someone or something he is not.

Look at the list of ideas you brainstormed on the "Getting Started" page. Choose the idea that you like best. Then write a plot outline based on the idea you've chosen on another sheet of paper.

CREATING CHARACTERS

HOW DO YOU CREATE CHARACTERS?

When you read a book, you may feel as if you know the characters; they may almost seem like real people. When this happens, it's because the author has shown you what the characters are like—friendly or shy or clever or funny. In a play, we learn about the characters from what they do and say, and from what other characters say about them. This means that when you write a play, you must have a clear picture of your characters in your mind; then the words they speak will fit their personalities and make them seem real.

Macmillan/McGraw-Hill

WHAT IS A CHARACTER SKETCH?

Most of the time, the characters in a play are people. If you
adapt a play from a folk tale such as "The Stonecutter," the
characters might also include animals or elements in nature,
such as a rock or the sun. No matter who the characters are,
it's important to give each one a personality. One way for you
to get a clear idea of each character's personality is to write
a character sketch. A character sketch describes the
character's appearance, friends, job, interests, and likes and
dislikes. Here's an example of a character sketch for the
stonecutter.

> The stonecutter is a small man who is very
> strong. He is dressed in simple clothes that
> are clean but worn. His hair is dark, and his
> skin is tanned from the sun. Wherever he goes,
> he carries a bag of heavy tools on his back. He
> is hardworking and knows his job. Because
> he is also honest and careful, he has many
> buyers for his stone. He lives by himself in a
> wooden hut. Although he is not rich, he has
> always been happy with what he has. He is a
> kind man who has lived a very simple life.

Look back at the plot you've outlined for your play. Make a
list of the main characters you will need to create. Then write
a short character sketch for each one. As you write your play,
keep your character sketches handy to remind you of what
each character is like. If you know your characters well, your
audience will get to know them, too.

A READERS THEATER SCRIPT

HOW DO I WRITE DIALOG FOR A SCRIPT?

Writing a play is different from writing a story. As you know, a play even looks different on the page. In a script, you'll find the names of the characters on the left side of the page, followed by a colon (:). The dialog, or the words spoken by a character, appears to the right of each character's name.

In a Readers Theater play, a narrator often appears as one of the characters. The narrator can describe a scene, tell when and where the scene is taking place, and describe action that can't be written as dialog. Here's part of a script for a Readers Theater adaptation of the folk tale described on the pages you've already completed.

> **Narrator:** One day, the stonecutter brought a stone to the home of a rich man. He could hardly believe what he saw! Beautiful carpets covered the floors. The furniture was made of polished wood. And hanging around the rich man's bed was a silk curtain tied back with gold tassels.
>
> **Stonecutter:** I never imagined that people lived like this! Ah, it must be wonderful to be rich.
>
> **Narrator:** The next morning, the stonecutter returned to his mountain. Now his bag felt heavy and his work seemed hard.

Macmillan/McGraw-Hill

Stonecutter: If only I were a rich man. I could sit on a satin chair. I could sleep in a bed with silk curtains and gold tassels. How happy I would be!

Narrator: No sooner had he spoken than a voice answered.

Spirit: Your wish has been heard. A rich man you shall be.

Narrator: The surprised stonecutter looked around, but there was no one in sight. He packed up his tools and started for home. When he arrived, he rubbed his eyes in wonder.

Use the dialog above to discuss these questions with a partner or in a small group.

- What are some possible differences between the script and a story-version of the same scene?
- How is the dialog set off?
- What kinds of information do you get from the narrator?
- Does the stonecutter's dialog sound the way you imagined it would?
- Who do you think will speak next?

Now it's your turn to write a scene for your play. Include dialog for the narrator and at least two other characters. Use the character sketches you created as a guide to how the characters would speak. Remember to use the narrator to set the scene and to describe actions that are not part of the dialog.

READY, SET, WRITE

This checklist will help guide you as you write your play. After you finish each step, put a check in the box.

Prewriting
☐ Brainstorm ideas for a play.
☐ Outline the plot.
☐ Write the character sketches.

Drafting
☐ Write a first draft of your play. If you work in a group, take turns recording sections of dialog as the group dictates it.
☐ Set up your script using play format. Write the names of the characters on the left and the dialog on the right. Skip a line between speakers.
☐ Use the narrator to describe actions that cannot be written as dialog and to tell about changes in time or place.
☐ Give your play a title.

Revising
☐ Reread your play. Check to be sure the story makes sense.
☐ Make sure the events are told in the right order.
☐ Check to see if the characters are believable.
☐ Add characters or take out characters if you need to.
☐ Read your play aloud. Change any dialog that does not sound natural.

Proofreading

☐ Correct all mistakes in spelling, grammar, punctuation, and script form.

☐ Ask someone else to check your script for mistakes you may have missed.

Publishing

☐ Make a final draft of your script. It should be neat and easy to read. Be sure that all the corrections have been made.

☐ Make a copy of the script for each member of the cast.

When your script is finished, it's time to start rehearsing your play. Keep an open mind—and an open ear—during the rehearsals. If you think something in the play could be improved, change it. When you're satisfied, it's on with the show! Don't forget to take a bow for all your work as author!

Choral Reading
Blocking Diagrams

Level 11/Unit 1
Goblin Feet

Level 11/Unit 2
THE SNOWFLAKE

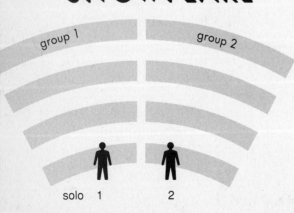

Level 11/Unit 2
Today

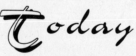

Level 11/Unit 3
Measure Me, Sky
YOUTH

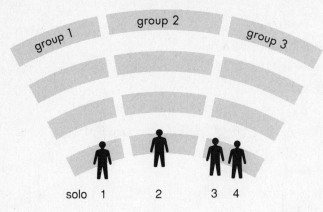

group 1 group 2 group 3

solo 1 2 3 4

Level 11/Unit 4
Writers

group 1 group 2

Level 11/Unit 5
CROSSING

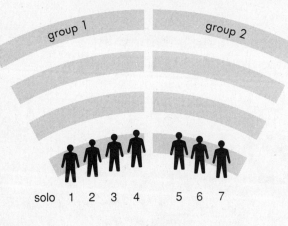

group 1 group 2

solo 1 2 3 4 5 6 7

Level 11/Unit 6
A Cliché

group 1 group 2

solo 1 2 3 4

Goblin Feet

Group 1: I am off down the road
Where the fairy lanterns glowed
And the little pretty flitter-mice are flying:
Group 2: A slender band of gray
It runs creepily away
And the the hedges and the grasses are a-sighing.
Group 3: The air is full of wings,
And of blundery beetle-things
That warn you with their whirring and their humming.
Group 4: O! I hear the tiny horns
Of enchanted leprechauns
And the padded feet of many gnomes a-coming!

Solo 1: O! the lights!
Solo 2: O! the gleams!
Solo 3: O! the little tinkly sounds!
Solo 4: O! the rustle of their noiseless little robes!
Solo 5: O! the echo of their feet—of their happy little feet!
Solo 6: O! their swinging lamps in little starlit globes.

Macmillan/McGraw-Hill

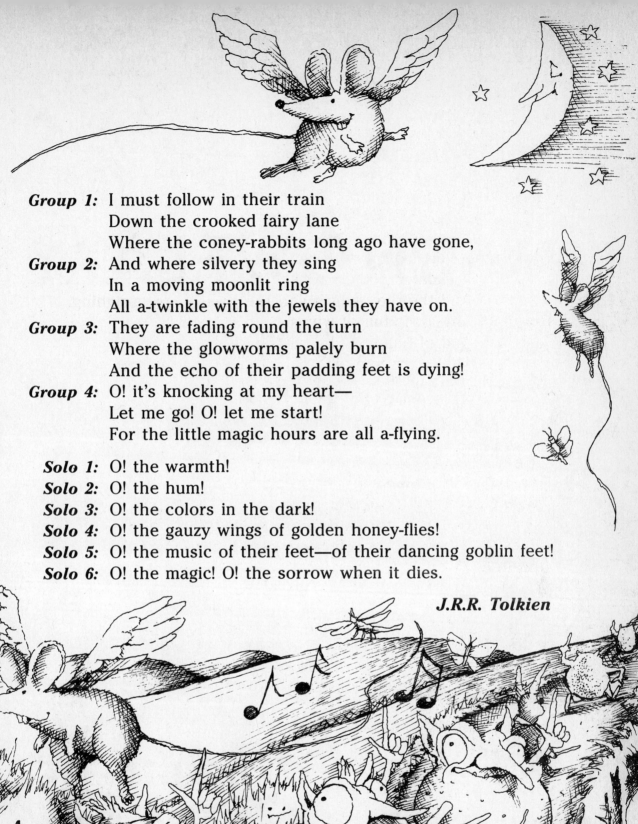

Group 1: I must follow in their train
Down the crooked fairy lane
Where the coney-rabbits long ago have gone,
Group 2: And where silvery they sing
In a moving moonlit ring
All a-twinkle with the jewels they have on.
Group 3: They are fading round the turn
Where the glowworms palely burn
And the echo of their padding feet is dying!
Group 4: O! it's knocking at my heart—
Let me go! O! let me start!
For the little magic hours are all a-flying.

Solo 1: O! the warmth!
Solo 2: O! the hum!
Solo 3: O! the colors in the dark!
Solo 4: O! the gauzy wings of golden honey-flies!
Solo 5: O! the music of their feet—of their dancing goblin feet!
Solo 6: O! the magic! O! the sorrow when it dies.

J.R.R. Tolkien

THE SNOWFLAKE

Solo 1: Before I melt,
Come, look at me!
Solo 2: This lovely icy filigree!
Group 1: Of a great forest
In one night
I make a wilderness
Of white:
Group 2: By skyey cold
Of crystals made,
All softly, on
Your finger laid,
Solo 1: I pause, that you
My beauty see:
Solo 2: Breathe, and I vanish
Instantly.

Walter de la Mare

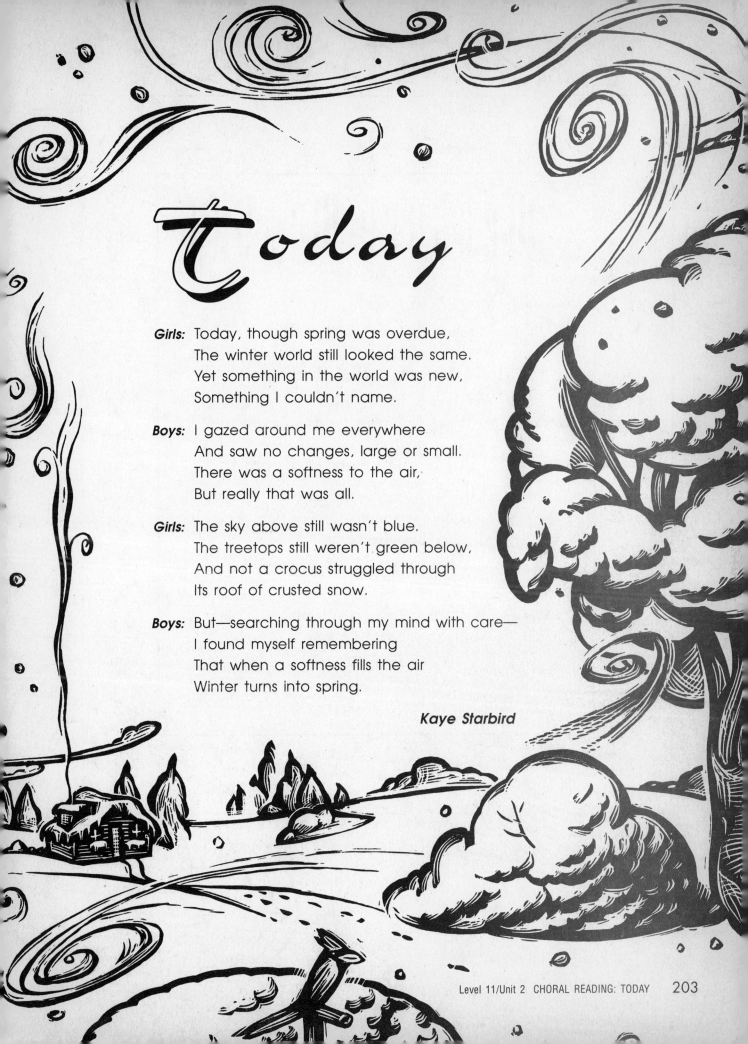

Today

Girls: Today, though spring was overdue,
The winter world still looked the same.
Yet something in the world was new,
Something I couldn't name.

Boys: I gazed around me everywhere
And saw no changes, large or small.
There was a softness to the air,
But really that was all.

Girls: The sky above still wasn't blue.
The treetops still weren't green below,
And not a crocus struggled through
Its roof of crusted snow.

Boys: But—searching through my mind with care—
I found myself remembering
That when a softness fills the air
Winter turns into spring.

Kaye Starbird

Measure Me, Sky

Solo 1: Measure me, sky!
Group 1:   Tell me I reach by a song
Nearer the stars;
    I have been little so long.

Solo 2: Weigh me, high wind!
Group 2:   What will your wild scales record?
Profit of pain,
    Joy by the weight of a word.

Solo 3: Horizon, reach out!
Group 3:   Catch at my hands, stretch me taut,
Rim of the world:
    Widen my eyes by a thought.

Solo 1: Sky, be my depth,
Solo 2:   Wind, be my width and my height,
Solo 3: World, my heart's span;
Solo 4:   Loveliness, wings for my flight.

Leonora Speyer

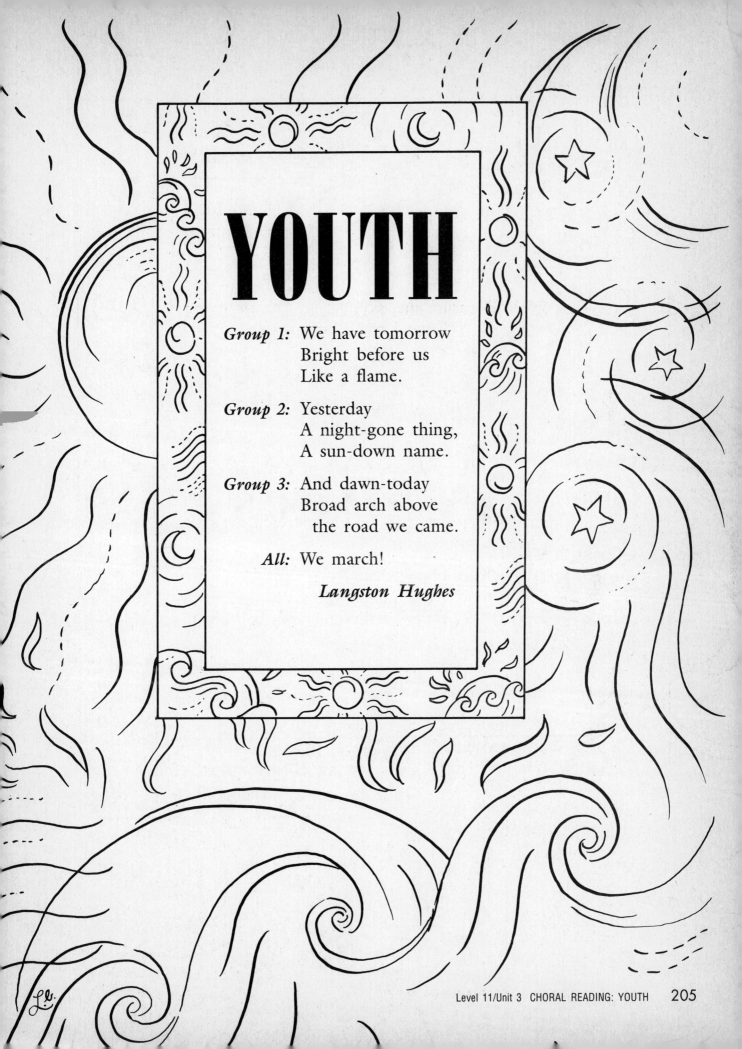

YOUTH

Group 1: We have tomorrow
Bright before us
Like a flame.

Group 2: Yesterday
A night-gone thing,
A sun-down name.

Group 3: And dawn-today
Broad arch above
the road we came.

All: We march!

Langston Hughes

Writers

Group 1: Emily writes of poetic things
Like crocuses and hummingbirds' wings,
Group 2: But I think people beat hummingbirds every time.

Group 1: Emily likes to write of snow
And dawn and candlelight aglow,
Group 2: But I'd rather write about me and Emily and stuff like that.

Group 2: The funny thing is, I delight
To read what Emily likes to write,
Group 1: And Emily says she thinks my poems are okay too.

Group 1: Also, sometimes, we switch with each other.
Emily writes of a fight with her mother.
Group 2: I tell about walking alone by the river,
—how still and golden it was.

Group 2: I know what Emily means, you see,
And, often, Emily's halfway me. . . .
Group 1: Oh, there's just no way to make anybody else understand.

Group 1: We're not a bit the same and yet,
We're closer than most people get.
Group 2: There's no one word for it. We just care about each other
the way we are supposed to.

Group 2: So I can look through Emily's eyes
Group 1: And she through mine.
All: It's no surprise,
When you come right down to it, that we're friends.

Jean Little

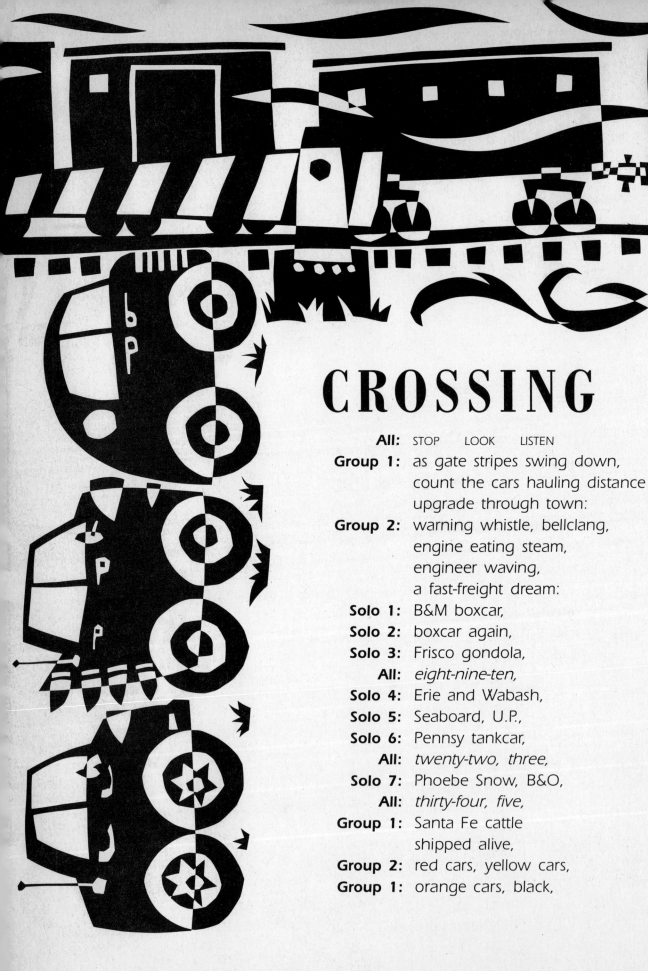

CROSSING

All: STOP   LOOK   LISTEN

Group 1: as gate stripes swing down,
count the cars hauling distance
upgrade through town:

Group 2: warning whistle, bellclang,
engine eating steam,
engineer waving,
a fast-freight dream:

Solo 1: B&M boxcar,

Solo 2: boxcar again,

Solo 3: Frisco gondola,

All: *eight-nine-ten,*

Solo 4: Erie and Wabash,

Solo 5: Seaboard, U.P.,

Solo 6: Pennsy tankcar,

All: *twenty-two, three,*

Solo 7: Phoebe Snow, B&O,

All: *thirty-four, five,*

Group 1: Santa Fe cattle
shipped alive,

Group 2: red cars, yellow cars,

Group 1: orange cars, black,

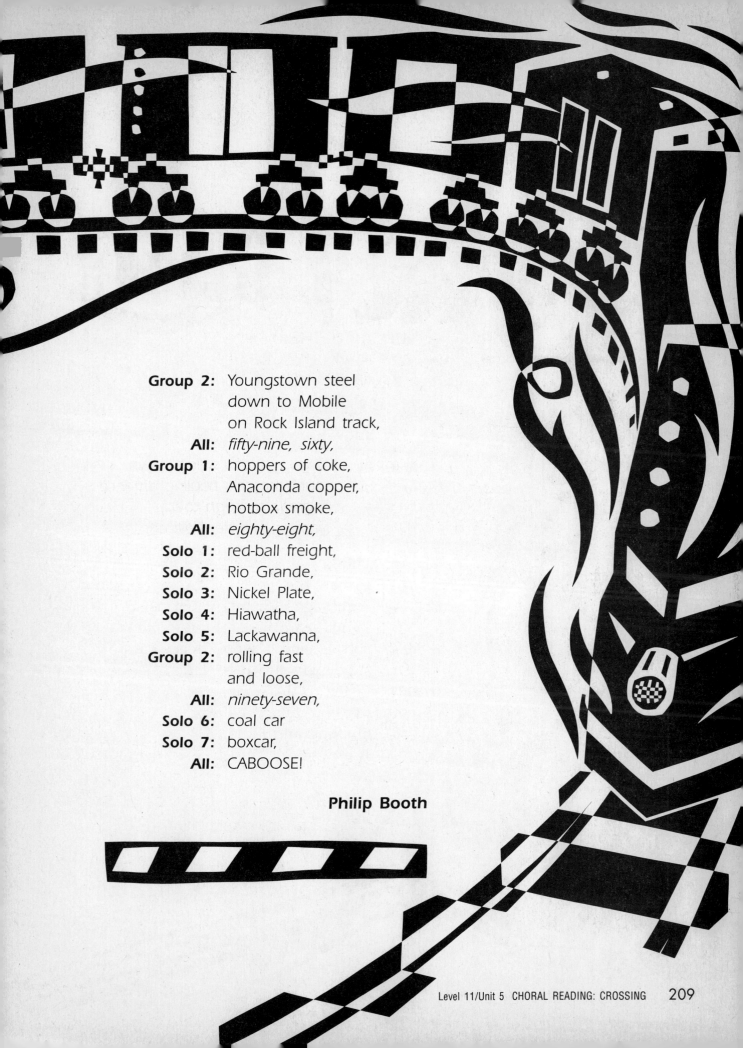

Group 2: Youngstown steel
down to Mobile
on Rock Island track,
All: *fifty-nine, sixty,*
Group 1: hoppers of coke,
Anaconda copper,
hotbox smoke,
All: *eighty-eight,*
Solo 1: red-ball freight,
Solo 2: Rio Grande,
Solo 3: Nickel Plate,
Solo 4: Hiawatha,
Solo 5: Lackawanna,
Group 2: rolling fast
and loose,
All: *ninety-seven,*
Solo 6: coal car
Solo 7: boxcar,
All: CABOOSE!

Philip Booth

A Cliché

All: A CLICHÉ

Group 1: is what we all say
when we're too lazy
to find another way

All: and so we say

Solo 1: *warm as toast,*

Solo 2: *quiet as a mouse,*

Solo 3: *slow as molasses,*

Solo 4: *quick as a wink.*

All: Think.

Solo 1: Is toast the warmest thing you know?

All: Think again, it might not be so.
Think again: it might even be snow!

Group 2: Soft as lamb's wool, fleecy snow,
a lacy shawl of new-fallen snow.

Group 1: Listen to that mouse go
scuttling and clawing,
nibbling and pawing.
A mouse can speak
if only a squeak.

Solo 2: Is a mouse the quietest thing you know?
All: Think again, it might not be so.
Think again: it might be a shadow.
Group 2: Quiet as a shadow,
quiet as growing grass,
quiet as a pillow,
or a looking glass.

Solo 3: *Slow as molasses,*
Solo 4: *quick as a wink.*
All: Before you say so,
take time to think.

Group 1: Slow as time passes
when you're sad and alone;
Group 2: quick as an hour can go
happily on your own.

Eve Merriam

PERFORMANCE
Evaluation

As a performer in Readers Theater, you may think of yourself as a reader. But you are a listener and a team member, too. Your performance in all three areas helps to make the production successful.

Use this sheet to help you evaluate your performance in each area.

	ALWAYS	MOST OF THE TIME	SOMETIMES	ALMOST NEVER	NEVER
## Oral-Reading Skills			3	4	5
Did I read my lines fluently?	1	2	3	4	5
Did I look up the pronunciation of unfamiliar words?	1	2	3	4	5
Did I mark my script for pauses and special emphasis?	1	2	3	4	5
Did I read with expression?	1	2	3	4	5
Did I read at the correct rate?	1	2	3	4	5
Did I pronounce the beginnings and endings of words clearly?	1	2	3	4	5
Did I project my voice?	1	2	3	4	5
Did I know my script well enough so I could look up as I read?	1	2	3	4	5
## Listening Skills					
Did I listen attentively for my cues and come in on time?	1	2	3	4	5
Did I listen to myself as I read and make adjustments if necessary?	1	2	3	4	5
Did I listen attentively as others read?	1	2	3	4	5
Did I try to visualize the action and setting?	1	2	3	4	5
## Teamwork Skills					
Did I come to my team prepared to contribute?	1	2	3	4	5
Did I take turns, allowing others to express themselves?	1	2	3	4	5
Did I show respect for others?	1	2	3	4	5
Did I make constructive suggestions to others?	1	2	3	4	5
Did I consider others' suggestions?	1	2	3	4	5

Describe one suggestion you used that came from a teammate.

Explain how this suggestion helped you improve your performance.

Select a personal goal for your next production and write about it.

Select a team goal for your next production and write about it.